Writers' Guide

to Strunk and White

Peggy M. Houghton, Ph.D.
Timothy J. Houghton, Ph.D.

Michele M. Pratt, Editor

Education is one of the best investments you will ever make…and our books maximize that investment!

Houghton & Houghton

ISBN: 978-1-935356-62-2

For order information, refer to Amazon.com.

Manufactured in the United States of America

Contents

Preface

Strunk & White: The Elements of Style is the premier reference book for writers. To further expand upon and provide better understanding of the various rules within the book, Houghton & Houghton have developed *Writers' Guide to Strunk & White*.

Our handbook highlights Strunk and White's foundational aspects using examples that clarify and add meaning to the book's rules and guidelines. In addition to expanding on punctuation and grammatical standards, examples are included for each respective rule. Even more useful are the short essays that demonstrate how these rules are used in written papers. Finally, a "Bonus Section" details how to set up a paper utilizing the American Psychological Association (APA) writing style.

Writers' Guide to Strunk & White will prove to be an invaluable resource for professional and academic writers. Use the rules and examples included and feel confident in your writing journey. We look forward to your success!

Part I: Basic Rules of Usage

Apostrophes

Apostrophes are used to show that a noun or an indefinite pronoun (*someone, somebody, anyone, anything, no one*) is possessive. Apostrophes are also used to show that one or more letters are missing from a contraction, as in *can't, don't, won't, I'm,* and *isn't.*

Possessive

In general, an apostrophe indicates possession or ownership.

To show ownership of nouns not ending in *s*, use *'s*. For nouns ending in *s*, use *'s* if the noun is singular (the business's system) but use only an apostrophe if the noun is plural (six months' leave).

> *Brent's* car was involved in a car accident last evening. (Brent = singular)
>
> At this point, it is *anyone's* game. (anyone = singular)
>
> The *truck's* engine was overheated. (truck = singular)
>
> The *trucks'* engines were too small for the job. (trucks = plural)
>
> After the final victory, the *boys'* jerseys were thrown throughout the locker room. (boys = plural)

This explanation and additional examples further explain Strunk & White's Chapter I (Rule #1).

Note: Possessive personal pronouns (*hers, his, its, ours, yours, theirs*) do not require an apostrophe.

Contractions

A contraction is a word in which an apostrophe takes the place of one or more letters. Contractions are used quite frequently in everyday conversation and are also used in informal writing. Common contractions include *can't* (cannot), *don't* (do not), *I'm* (I am), *isn't* (is not), *it's* (it is), *let's* (let us), *they're* (they are), *wasn't* (was not), *weren't* (were not), *we've* (we have), *who's* (who is), *won't* (will not), and *you're* (you are).

Regardless of the weather, *I'm* going to the baseball game tonight. (I'm = I am)

It's not going to be pretty! (It's = It is)

Commas

Commas separate sentence parts clearly. Without properly placed commas, many sentences are confusing and difficult to understand. Some people think that a comma should be inserted whenever the writer pauses to think or take a breath before continuing a sentence. This is true in some cases, but it is not a reliable rule. Commas serve several distinct functions in writing, and there are different rules for each of these functions. Some specific rules are explained and illustrated below.

This explanation and additional examples further explain Strunk & White's Chapter I (Rule #2).

Series

Three or more items listed within a sentence are considered a series. Whenever a sentence contains a series of items, place a comma after each element (prior to the conjunction...*and, but, or, etc.*) within the series.

> Today I plan to exercise, shop for groceries, cut the grass, and prepare our dinner. (*Exercise, grocery shop, cut the grass*, and *prepare our dinner* is a series. Commas are required after each element within the series. Be certain that the comma is placed before the conjunction...*and* in this example.)
>
> Shall we bake, grill, or fry the chicken? (*Bake, grill,* or *fry* is a series. Commas are required after each element within the series. Be certain that the comma is placed before the conjunction...*or* in this example.)

Note: Two items do not constitute a series, and they do not require a comma.

> Reading and writing are taught in grade school. (Because there are only two items in this series, *reading* and *writing*, a comma is not required.)

Parenthetical expressions between commas (Restrictive versus Nonrestrictive Elements)

Restrictive elements in a sentence are essential to the actual meaning of the sentence. Restrictive elements, therefore, are not set off with commas because they are required in order to understand the complete meaning. Nonrestrictive elements, however, are not essential to the actual meaning of the sentence. They are not needed in order to understand the context of the sentence, so they are set off with commas.

This explanation and additional examples further explain Strunk & White's Chapter I (Rule #3).

> Restrictive: Academic institutions that are not for profit do not have to file certain tax forms. (The phrase *that are not for profit* is essential to the meaning of this sentence, so it is not set off with commas.)

This explanation and additional examples further explain Strunk & White's Chapter I (Rule #3).

Restrictive: Politicians who do not have to run for re-election are much more likely to vote for the essential budget cuts. (The phrase *who do not have to run for re-election* is essential to the meaning of the sentence, so it is not set off with commas.)

Nonrestrictive: My favorite day of the week, Saturday, is for relaxing and having fun. (*Saturday* is an appositive, or word renaming the day, and is not essential to the meaning of the sentence. Therefore, it is set off with commas.)

Nonrestrictive: I will, however, need to acquire business experience. (The transition, *however*, is not essential to the meaning of the sentence. Therefore, it is set off with commas.)

Dates

In dates indicated by month, day, and year, use a comma after the day (and after the year, if there is no other punctuation). In dates indicated by only a month and a year, or a month and a day, do not use a comma. Also, do not use a comma in dates written in military fashion (day, month, year).

December 7, 1941, is a date that will always be remembered. (A comma is required after the day and year because the month, day, and year are specified.)

December 1941 was the month the Japanese attacked Pearl Harbor. (No comma is required because only the month and year are specified.)

December 7 is a date that will always be associated with Pearl Harbor. (No comma is required because only the month and day are specified.)

The attack was set for 7 December 1941. (No comma is required because this date is written in military fashion.)

Abbreviations

An *abbreviation* is a shortened version of a word or group of words. Generally speaking, you should use abbreviations sparingly when writing. Too many abbreviations result in a choppy writing style. Consequently, the reader has difficulty understanding the meaning of the sentence. Only use an abbreviation if you are using a word or group of words more than once within the writing. When an abbreviation is appropriate, spell out the entire word or group of words the first time it is used, followed by the abbreviation placed within parentheses. A comprehensive list of abbreviation rules is reviewed below.

Titles (before and after names)

Whenever an abbreviated title immediately precedes a proper name (*Dr. Walter Reed, Gen. Dwight D. Eisenhower*), the title is capitalized. If there is no proper name after the title (I need a doctor. Ask the general.), it does not get capitalized and is not abbreviated.

When an abbreviated title follows a proper name (*George Adams, M.D., Mary Jones, M.A.*), the title must be capitalized.

> He couldn't understand the problem, even though he was an M.D.

There is some disagreement among scholars about academic and professional titles. The traditional method is to use periods after each initial; but in today's world, the periods are often omitted. It appears that both ways are proper. The examples below illustrate the traditional method of punctuating titles with periods. Whichever method is used, it's important to be consistent.

> *Marie Phillips, Ph.D.,* addressed the graduating class.
>
> *Joseph Knoll Jr.* recently wed *Dr. Mary Sanders.*
>
> The teacher earned a *B.A., M.A.,* and *Ph.D.*

Time

When words and numbers are used together, the abbreviation rules discussed above still apply. The accepted rule for time is that you can use either capital letters without periods (*AM/PM*) or lowercase letters with periods (*a.m./p.m.*). You should not use abbreviations with the term *o'clock*. To differentiate morning from evening with this term, you should write *seven o'clock in the morning* or *seven o'clock in the evening*. Any time a sentence ends with an abbreviation, the period from the abbreviation is considered the ending punctuation of the sentence.

The play will begin at 7:00 *p.m.* sharp.

We should probably leave our house at 6:15 *PM* to get seated in time.

We're supposed to be there at *six o'clock in the morning*.

Countries

Abbreviations used for the names of countries, nations, cities, and counties are always capitalized. The first time a country is used in writing, it should be spelled out. The abbreviated form should be placed in parentheses after the country. Subsequent listings of the country can be written in its abbreviated format. The names of states should never be abbreviated except in mailing addresses, and then both letters are capitalized.

I do not support that section of our *U.S.* foreign policy. (United States)

I have visited the *U.K.* several times. (United Kingdom)

Send it to J. Hancock, 1245 Main Street, Lansing, *MI.* (Michigan)

Corporations

When initials are used to abbreviate the name of a company or corporation, they are always capitalized and no periods are needed.

NBC (National Broadcasting Company)

KFC (Kentucky Fried Chicken)

IBM (International Business Machines)

Institutions

When initials are used to abbreviate the name of an organization, or to abbreviate familiar phrases, they are always capitalized. Note that these initials do not require periods.

AAA (American Automobile Association)

APA (American Psychological Association)

MLA (Modern Language Association)

AKA (also known as)

PC (personal computer)

ABD (all but dissertation)

AWOL (absent without leave)

Common Latin terms

When abbreviations are used to indicate a common Latin phrase, they should not be capitalized. Such examples include *i.e.* (*id est*...that is), *e.g.* (*exempli gratia*...for example), *etc.* (*et cetera*...and so forth). These Latin terms should be italicized whenever they are used. Latin terms are generally followed by a comma; however, exceptions may apply based on context.

I never go to horror movies (*e.g., Halloween 13*), because they frighten me.

He was a numismatist (*i.e.,* coin collector) of great reputation.

Spacing and periods with abbreviated terms

Generally speaking, periods are used for lowercase abbreviations (such as *e.g.*). However, when citing a commonly known lowercase abbreviation (*mph*), no periods are required. Finally, when an abbreviation ends a sentence, the period that coincides with the abbreviation is also used to end the sentence.

Acronyms

Don't confuse acronyms and abbreviations. An acronym is usually formed by taking the first initials of a phrase or compound word group and using those initials to form a word that stands for something. Thus NATO, pronounced *natoh*, is an acronym for North Atlantic Treaty Organization, and LASER, pronounced *lazer*, is an acronym for Light Amplification by Stimulated Emission of Radiation. These acronyms are usually written in all upper case letters, but there are exceptions such as *scuba*, which is an acronym for Self-Contained Underwater Breathing Apparatus. In some cases, abbreviations and acronyms are used interchangeably. AARP, for example, is a set of initials which is sometimes spelled out and sometimes pronounced as *arp*.

It appears that there are no hard and fast rules for using periods in either acronyms or abbreviations. More and more, newspapers and journals seem to drop the periods (NAACP, NCAA, *etc.*). Consistency, obviously, is important.

This explanation and additional examples further explain Strunk & White's Chapter I (Rule #4).

Placement of a comma when a conjunction introduces an independent clause

An *independent clause* contains a subject and a verb and can stand alone as a simple sentence.

A comma should be used when a conjunction introduces an independent clause.

Since time was running short, we decided to drive rather than walk. (*Since time was running short* introduces the independent clause *we decided to drive rather than walk.*)

While I don't enjoy studying long hours, the sacrifice is well worth the time. (*While I don't enjoy studying long hours* introduces the independent clause *the sacrifice is well worth the time.*)

Two independent clauses connected by a conjunction

When two independent clauses are connected by a conjunction (*and, or, for, nor, but, so, yet*), a comma is required. Below are several examples of the correct use of commas and conjunctions:

My favorite sport is football, but I also like to play basketball. (*My favorite sport is football* is an independent clause; likewise, *I also like to play basketball* is independent. The coordinating conjunction *but* connects the two independent clauses, so a comma is placed before *but.*)

I don't like canned vegetables, nor do I like canned soups. (*I don't like canned vegetables* is an independent clause; likewise, *I like canned soups* is independent. The coordinating conjunction *nor* connects the two independent clauses, so a comma is placed before *nor.*)

Note: The comma is always placed *before* the conjunction, not after the conjunction. Also, sentences with compound verbs or compound subjects do not need a comma.

Janice *walked* and *danced* with great poise. (two verbs)

Janice and *Katherine* danced with great poise. (two subjects)

Conjunctions with only one independent clause

A comma and a conjunction are used only to separate two independent clauses. In cases where a conjunction is used with only one independent clause, a comma is not required. Below are examples of conjunctions where no comma is required:

> The train stopped at the station and slowly continued the journey. (*The train stopped at the station* is an independent clause. However, *slowly continued the journey* is not independent. Therefore, a comma is not required.)
>
> The new graduate nervously entered the conference room and prepared for his upcoming interview. (*The new graduate nervously entered the conference room* is an independent clause. However, *prepared for his upcoming interview* is not independent. Therefore, a comma is not required.)

Independent clauses are not joined with a comma

This explanation and additional examples further explain Strunk & White's Chapter I (Rule #5).

Two independent clauses cannot be connected with a comma alone. There must be a coordinating conjunction or a semicolon. When two independent clauses are connected with a comma, a *comma splice* results. Below is an example of a comma splice.

> Benjamin Franklin invented many things, one of his best inventions was the Franklin Stove. (There are two independent clauses here, and they cannot be connected with simply a comma. To correct the sentence, you have to add a semicolon or a conjunction such as *and* or *but* before the word *one*.)

Semicolons

A semicolon is a punctuation mark that can be used to connect two independent clauses that are closely related. The semicolon is used in place of a conjunction. Semicolons are also used when two independent clauses are connected with a transitional word (*however*, *therefore*, *etc.*). Note that when a transitional word is used, the semicolon is placed before the transitional word, and the comma is placed after the transitional word. Finally, a semicolon can also be used to replace a comma when a sentence contains a series where one element within the series already contains a comma or multiple commas. Some writers never use a semicolon because they prefer to break ideas into two separate sentences.

Semicolons between independent clauses

When two related independent clauses are connected without using a coordinating conjunction, a semicolon is placed between the two independent clauses. Here again, a period could be used. However, a semicolon indicates a close relationship between the two clauses.

I enjoy running outdoors; I do not enjoy running on a treadmill. (No coordinating conjunction is used between the closely related independent clauses; therefore, a semicolon is placed between the two clauses.)

Tina left the grocery market in a hurry; she wanted dinner ready before her guests arrived. (No coordinating conjunction is used between the closely related independent clauses; therefore, a semicolon is placed between the two clauses.)

Semicolons with a transitional word

If two independent clauses are connected with a transitional word (*i.e. however, therefore, etc.*), a semicolon is placed before the transitional word and a comma follows the transitional word.

My goal in life is to become an actress; however, I do not intend to become famous! (The transitional word, *however,* divides the two independent clauses. Note that the semicolon is placed before the transitional word, and the comma is placed after the transitional word.)

I intend to open a business and earn a good living with my knowledge of computers; therefore, I am taking several technology courses. (Again, the transitional word, *therefore,* divides the two independent clauses. Note that the semicolon is placed before the transitional word, and the comma is placed after the transitional word.)

Semicolons in place of commas

At times, one or more of the items in a series may contain a comma. When this happens, the series is divided by semicolons, not commas. Semicolons make it easier to identify each item, including items that contain commas.

My favorite vacation spots include Berlin, Germany; Florence, Italy; and London, England. (Each element in the series contains a comma; therefore, the series is separated with semicolons.)

I like to shop with my mother; my neighbor, Chris Thatcher; and my best friend, Kathleen Jacobs. (The last two items of the series include a comma; therefore, the entire series is separated with semicolons.)

Avoid breaking sentences into two sentences

When a period is erroneously used in place of a comma, the sentence appears awkward. To correct this problem, replace the period with a comma and change the subsequent word to lower case.

> Incorrect: Susan picked up the dog yesterday. After coming home from vacation.
>
> Correct: Susan picked up the dog yesterday, after coming home from vacation.
>
> Incorrect: Robert is a computer genius. A man with remarkable technological skills.
>
> Correct: Robert is a computer genius, a man with remarkable technological skills.

This explanation and additional examples further explain Strunk & White's Chapter I (Rule #6).

Occasionally, it is acceptable to use a period to create two sentences. This is used to signify emphasis. The technique should be used sparingly because it may cause the reader to believe the sentence is grammatically incorrect.

> The suspense continues. Everyone weary!

Colons

Use a colon after an independent clause introduces a list of specifics, an appositive, an emphasis, or an illustration.

Colons are generally used to indicate an introduction. A colon may be used to introduce a list, a quotation, or an appositive that contains an independent clause. A colon is placed after the words *as follows* or *the following*. Colons can also be used between two sentences, when the first sentence serves as an introduction to the second sentence.

When a list follows the words *as follows* or *the following*, a colon is placed after the words *as follows* or *the following*.

This explanation and additional examples further explain Strunk & White's Chapter I (Rule #7).

> My grocery list includes the following: bread, milk, and eggs.
>
> The workers' demands are as follows: higher wages, longer break times, and more vacation days.

Lists do not always begin with *as follows* or *the following*. When a list follows the words *such as*, *like*, or *including* a colon is not used.

> I try to avoid sweets such as cookies, candy, and ice cream.

A colon can also be used between two independent clauses, but only if the second clause clearly emphasizes or illustrates the first clause. This is a somewhat specialized use of a colon, and a period or semicolon would make more sense in most cases.

> My textbooks cost a fortune: All of my summer savings have evaporated! (The second independent clause *All of my summer savings have evaporated* clearly explains the first independent clause *My textbooks cost a fortune*.)

Note: The second clause may or may not begin with a capital letter. Whichever method you use, it's important to be consistent throughout your writing.

Other uses of colons include the following: between hours and minutes, after formal salutations, and to indicate ratios or proportions.

> We will meet at 5:00 p.m. sharp! (time)
>
> Dear Mr. Smith: (formal salutation in a letter)
>
> The faculty to student ratio is 1:5 in remedial courses. (ratio of faculty to students)

Dashes

Dashes are used to indicate an interruption, provide a long appositive, or denote a summary.

A dash can be used to add such things as examples, definitions, appositives, contrasts, asides, or suspense. Other punctuation marks can also serve these functions—but a dash is stronger than a comma and less formal than a colon. Colons and semicolons are generally used in formal writing. Dashes should be used sparingly.

> Childhood obesity is spiraling upward—tripling in the past 30 years. (*Tripling in the past 30 years* emphasizes *childhood obesity*.)
>
> Thousands of teenagers—12,625 to be exact—braved the frigid weather to secure tickets for the upcoming concert. (*12,625 to be exact* further clarifies the precise number of teenagers.)

This explanation and additional examples further explain Strunk & White's Chapter I (Rule #8).

Note: Use two hyphens to form a dash. Alternatively, some computer programs provide an *em dash*. The e*m dash* is acceptable as well.

Subject-Verb Agreement

The subject and verb must be in agreement.

Complete sentences must contain a subject and a verb. In addition, the subject and verb must be in agreement. They have to agree in *number* and *person*. *Person* is used with nouns and pronouns to show who or what is acting or experiencing an action. *First person* is the one speaking (*I, we*); *second person* is the one being spoken to (*you*); and *third person* is the person or thing spoken about (*he, she, it, they*).

In other words, the subject and verb must be parallel. If a singular subject is used, a singular verb must also be used. The

This explanation and additional examples further explain Strunk & White's Chapter I (Rule #9)

reverse is true as well. If a plural subject is used, a plural verb must be used.

Many sentences contain compound subjects, and quite often one of the subjects is singular and the other is plural. When subjects are joined by *or* or *nor*, the verb must agree with the subject that is closest to it.

> Neither the sheriff nor the officers were chasing the outlaws. (The verb *were chasing* is plural because *officers* is plural.)
>
> Neither the officers nor the sheriff was chasing the outlaws. (The verb *was chasing* is singular because *sheriff* is singular.)

Compound subjects joined by *and* usually take a plural verb, as shown in the second example below.

> Katherine runs errands every day after work. (*Katherine* is singular; *runs* is singular.)
>
> Peter and Michelle run errands every day after work. (*Peter and Michelle* are plural; *run* is plural.)
>
> A turtle traditionally moves slowly. (*Turtle* is singular; *moves* is singular.)
>
> Turtles traditionally move slowly. (*Turtles* are plural; *move* is plural.)

Sometimes subjects are considered *collective nouns*. These types of subjects are words used to describe a group of nouns. Examples include *team, crowd,* and *army.* When these types of subjects are used, they are considered singular because they function as a singular unit. Therefore, a collective noun uses a singular verb or pronoun.

> The team plays every game as if it were the season's final effort. (*Team* is a singular collective noun; therefore, *plays* is singular.)
>
> The committee has reached a decision. (*Committee* is a singular collective noun; therefore, *has reached* is singular.)

Indefinite pronouns replace nouns without specifying which noun they replace. Most indefinite pronouns are singular. These include *another, anybody, anyone, each, either, everybody, everyone, everything, little, much, neither, nobody, no one, nothing, one, other, somebody, someone,* and *something.* Plural indefinite pronouns include *both, few, many, others,* and *several.* There are also a few indefinite pronouns which can be singular or plural, depending on how they are used. These pronouns are *all, any, more, most, none,* and *some.*

> The coaches or team captain determines who rides the bus. (*Captain* is singular and closest to the verb, so the verb *determines* is singular.)
>
> Neither my sister nor my brothers are going to the game. (*Brothers* is plural and closest to the verb; therefore, the plural verb *are going* is used.).

Proper pronoun case

Case refers to the form of a pronoun that shows how it is functioning in a given sentence. Depending on context, pronouns can function as a subject, an object, or a possessive. Personal pronouns refer to a particular person or thing. They include *I, you, he, she, it, we,* and *they.*

There are three types of pronoun cases: subjective, objective, and possessive. In the *subjective case,* the pronoun is used as the subject of the sentence. In the *objective case,* pronouns are used as objects of prepositions or verbs. Finally, in the *possessive case,* pronouns are used to show possession or ownership.

Review the following table, which shows personal pronouns in all three cases.

SUBJECTIVE	OBJECTIVE	POSSESSIVE
I	me	my/mine
you	you	your/yours
he	him	his
she	her	her/hers
it	it	its
we	us	our/ours
they	them	their/theirs
who	whom	whose

Note the following commonly used pronouns along with their respective definitions. Examples of each pronoun usage appear below the definition.

Its versus It's

Its shows possession. *It's* is a contraction for *it is*.

> The dog wagged *its* tail. (The tail belongs [possession] to the dog.)
>
> The bright sunshine caused the area rug to lose *its* color. (The color belongs [possession] to the area rug.)
>
> *It's* a difficult problem to resolve. (*It's* is a contraction for *it is*.)
>
> *It's* the wedding of the century! (*It's* is a contraction for *it is*.)

Whom versus Who

Who should be used as the subject of a sentence or a subordinate clause.

> *Who* is going to the party this Saturday? (*Who* is the subject of the sentence.)
>
> Meredith is the woman *who* is wearing black. (*Who* is the subject of a subordinate clause.)

Whom is used as the object of a verb or after a preposition.

> To *whom* do I owe my gratitude? *(Whom* is the object of a preposition.)
>
> The lost diamond belongs to *whom*? (*Whom* is the object of a verb.)

Their versus There versus They're

These three words are pronounced exactly the same, but they have completely different meanings. *Their* is a possessive pronoun used to show plural ownership. *There* is a specific place. *They're* is a contraction for *they are.*

> *Their* car was stolen last week. (*Their* is a plural possessive meaning the car belonging to those people.)

> The theft happened over *there*. (*There* denotes a specific place where the theft occurred.)
>
> *They're* quite sure the theft was pre-planned. (*They're* is a contraction for *they are*.)

Who's versus Whose

These are two words that are pronounced alike but have different meanings. *Who's* is a contraction for *who is*. *Whose* is a pronoun and the possessive form of *who*. Both words are used quite often in questions.

> *Who's* the gal in the long red dress? (*Who's* is a contraction for *who is*.)
>
> Robert is the man *who's* responsible for the garden. (*Who's* is a contraction for *who is*.)
>
> I wonder *whose* horse will win the race? (*Whose* is a possessive referring to several different owners or riders.)
>
> Mary is the student *whose* behavior earned her the award. (*Whose* is a possessive referring to Mary.)

Your versus You're

Your is a possessive pronoun and shows ownership. *You're* is a contraction for *you are*.

> *Your* time is coming to an end. (*Your* is a possessive pronoun.)
>
> What is *your* estimated time of arrival? (*Your* is a possessive pronoun.)
>
> *You're* one of the finest card players I have ever encountered! (*You're* is a contraction for *you are*.)
>
> *You're* going to win the top prize! (*You're* is a contraction for *you are*.)

Participial Phrase

Participial phrases must clearly refer to the subject to which they modify.

A participle is a verb type that includes the participle and its respective modifiers and/or complements. When a participial phrase is used to begin a sentence, it must clearly refer to the subject.

Incorrect: After trying out for the football team, the coach encouraged the student to elevate his grade point average. (This example implies that the *coach* decided to try out for the football team.)

Correct: After trying out for the football team, the student was encouraged by the coach to elevate his grade point average. (This properly worded sentence correctly indicates that the *student* decided to try out for the football team...not the coach.)

Incorrect: Before leaving the Halloween party, a scary ghost jumped out at Maggie. (This example is confusing because it implies that a *scary ghost* was leaving the Halloween party.)

Correct: Before leaving the Halloween party, Maggie was startled by a scary ghost. (This example clearly illustrates that it was *Maggie* who was startled by the ghost as she was leaving the Halloween party.)

Incorrect: While studying for my final exam, my coffee spilled all over the table. (This example is also confusing because it incorrectly implies that the *coffee* was studying for a final exam.)

Correct: While studying for my final exam, I spilled my coffee all over the table. (This example clearly indicates that it was *I* who was studying for the final exam...not the coffee.)

Incorrect: After being released from prison, the judge ordered the convicted felon to wear a tether for six months. (The above example implies that the *judge* was released from prison.)

Correct: After being released from prison, the convicted felon was ordered by the judge to wear a tether for six months. (This properly worded sentence correctly indicates that the *convicted felon* was ordered to wear the tether...not the judge.)

This explanation and additional examples further explain Strunk & White's Chapter I (Rule #11).

In addition to phrases that begin a sentence, all other types of phrases must clearly modify, or explain, the intended word, phrase, or clause within the sentence. When a modifier is placed inappropriately, the sentence appears awkward and confusing. The best way to ensure understanding is to place the modifier right next to the word or words it modifies. Otherwise, the sentence structure may result in confusion and misunderstanding.

Incorrect: When Peter arrived at the race track, the car he had built loudly announced its arrival. (This sentence implies that *Peter had built the car loudly*.)

Correct: When Peter arrived at the race track, the car he had built announced its arrival loudly. (This sentence correctly implies that *the car Peter had built was loud*.)

Incorrect: The handsome young man was distributing newspapers in a bathing suit. (This sentence implies that *the newspapers were in a bathing suit*!)

Correct: The handsome young man in a bathing suit distributed newspapers. (This sentence correctly implies that *the young man was wearing the bathing suit*.)

Other commonly misplaced modifiers include words such as *only*, *even*, *almost*, *nearly*, *often*, and *just*.

Part II: Principles of Composition

Style and design consistency

Choose and maintain an acceptable style and design

Writing styles are the way in which writers assemble words and sentences. Just like no two people are alike, no two writing styles are alike as well. All writers choose a different type of format or design style. While writing styles and design are unique, they should be geared toward the type of writing being conveyed. Sometimes concise and to-the-point writing is appropriate, as in quick email correspondence. Other times, more sophisticated flowery language is more suitable for the design...such as in poetry. A seasoned writer analyzes the intended content to be conveyed and then determines the appropriate design. Once the design is chosen, it is the writer's responsibility not to deviate from the design throughout the entire writing.

This explanation and additional examples further explain Strunk & White's Chapter II (Rule #12).

Topic sentences and paragraphs: Development of composition

Topic sentences and paragraphs

A topic sentence states the main idea of a paragraph. It identifies the subject matter and provides direction for all other sentences in the paragraph.

Topic sentences typically are placed at the beginning of a paragraph. Readers generally look at the first few sentences

This explanation and additional examples further explain Strunk & White's Chapter II (Rule #13).

of a paragraph to get an idea about the subject matter. Topic sentences alert readers to the most important points of an essay and provide an outline of the pending statements. In summary, an appropriate topic sentence makes a claim about the subject matter, unifies the paragraph, and is clear and concise.

Canada is a great country for vacationing. There are hundreds of lakes, and much of the countryside is virtually unchanged by man. Big cities such as Toronto and Montreal offer world-renowned attractions that compete with any major metropolitan area in the world. Canada is an obvious choice for vacationing people looking for urban or rural beauty.

(*Canada is a great country for vacationing* is the topic sentence. The remaining sentences support the idea.)

This explanation and additional examples further explain Strunk & White's Chapter II (Rule #13).

A paragraph is a distinct section of writing that discusses single themes or areas of thought. It should contain one or more sentences and is typically indicated by indentation or a new line. However, single sentence paragraphs are a rare exception and should only be sparingly used. Paragraphs use related sentences to discuss a single topic and offer support for the main idea, or topic sentence.

Well written paragraphs flow logically and seamlessly into each other. Poorly written paragraphs result in reader confusion and loss of interest in the subject matter.

Incorrect (one paragraph):

Baseball is a good sport for spectators who like to be outdoors. Most games are played on a field in an open-air stadium with complete exposure to everything Mother Nature has to offer. Game outcomes can be influenced by the weather, which is favored by those who prefer games that are played under natural conditions. Basketball is geared more toward people who enjoy games from the comforts of a climate controlled building. The temperature during every game is relatively the same, regardless of the conditions outside. Climate does not affect the outcome of a game, and this is preferred by those who enjoy seeing games played under optimal conditions. *(Notice how the two topics within the paragraph run together creating reader confusion.)*

Correct (two paragraphs)

Baseball is a good sport for spectators who like to be outdoors. Most games are played on a field in an open-air stadium with complete exposure to everything Mother Nature has to offer. Game outcomes can be influenced by the weather, which is favored by those who prefer games that are played under natural conditions.

Basketball is geared more toward people who enjoy games from the comforts of a climate controlled building. The temperature during every game is relatively the same, regardless of the conditions outside. Climate does not affect the outcome of a game, and this is preferred by those who enjoy seeing games played under optimal conditions. *(Notice how the transition from one paragraph to the next is logical and easy to follow. Also, notice how a new topic starts a new paragraph.)*

Writing language

Active/Passive Voice

Verbs can be in either the *active* or the *passive* voice. *Voice* indicates how the subject relates to the action expressed by the verb. In the active voice, the subject actually performs the action of the verb. With active sentences, the thing performing the action is the subject of the sentence and the thing receiving the action is the object. In the passive voice, the subject is the recipient of the action. With passive sentences, the thing receiving the action is the subject of the sentence and the thing performing the action is generally located near the end of the sentence.

Consider the following active and passive sentences:

This explanation and additional examples further explain Strunk & White's Chapter II (Rule #14).

> Active: Stanley considers all power tools to be labor-savers. (This is an *active* sentence because Stanley is performing the action of considering.)
>
> Passive: All power tools are considered labor-savers by Stanley. (This is a *passive* sentence because Stanley is performing the action but is located at the end of the sentence.)
>
> Active: Martin replaced the dying tree. (This is an *active* sentence because Martin is performing the action of replacing.)
>
> Passive: The dying tree was replaced by Martin. (This is a *passive* sentence because Martin is performing the action but is located at the end of the sentence.)
>
> Active: Sandra arranged the dinner location and reservations. (This is an *active* sentence because Sandra is performing the action of arranging.)
>
> Passive: The dinner location and reservations were arranged by Sandra. (This is a *passive* sentence because Sandra is performing the action but is located at the end of the sentence.)

While both forms of voice are utilized in writing, active voice is recommended whenever possible. Active voice strengthens the writing and makes the author appear confident. Passive voice often requires sentence constructions that may appear awkward or stilted, although there are times when it is useful. Writing in *all* active or *all* passive voice results in choppy and mundane reading. The challenge for the writer is to balance the use of both styles.

Positive Writing

Write in a positive tone

Writing tone affects the writer's message as well as the way in which the reader interprets the writing. There are three types of tones: neutral, negative, and positive.

Neutral writing essentially shows no emotion. While it is not negative in nature, it is not positive either. This type of writing can sometimes come across as cold or harsh. It actually depends on the reader's attitude at the given time of reading. Because of the potential for misinterpretation, this style should be avoided in scholarly writing.

Negative writing, as the name implies, uses pessimistic language. This style may come across as rude or belligerent. This type of writing can prove to be detrimental to the writer and, therefore, its use is strongly discouraged. When negative information needs to be conveyed, try to change the wording to a positive tone.

Positive writing is, obviously, writing that incorporates positive language. It creates optimism and entices the reader to continue reading. This type of writing perks the emotions of the reader and provides a sense of encouragement. It is the style that is highly recommended for all types of writing.

Specific techniques can create positive language. One way to create a positive environment is to avoid the use of negative words. Care should be taken to focus on the positive…not the negative. Words such as *unfortunately*, *don't*, and *reject* create

This explanation and additional examples further explain Strunk & White's Chapter II (Rule #15).

a negative tone. Instead of using any type of negative word, revise the sentence and provide a positive slant.

> Incorrect: We do not accept Discover. (*Not* is a negative word and should be replaced with a positive term.)
>
> Correct: We gladly accept Visa and MasterCard. (*Gladly* replaces *not* and provides a more positive tone.)

Another technique to avoid negativism is to focus on the solution…not the problem. This deemphasizes what can't be done and emphasizes what can and will be done.

> Incorrect: Unfortunately, the person you need to speak to is not available. (*Unfortunately* and *not* are negative words and should be replaced with more appealing terms.)
>
> Correct: The employee you need to speak with will be more than willing to assist you on Monday. (Creates a positive tone.)

This explanation and additional examples further explain Strunk & White's Chapter II (Rule #16).

Using definitive, specific, and concrete language

Specific versus abstract writing

The purpose of writing is to share thoughts and ideas with others. In order to do this effectively, you need to write with words that are definitive, specific, concrete, and clear. There is no body language (nonverbal cues) of any kind to assist your reader with the meaning of the intended writing. The only tools to use are words.

> Incorrect: A large sum of money was found in the wealthy senior woman's wallet. (This sentence uses vague terms to define *large sum* and *wealthy senior*.)
>
> Correct: One thousand dollars was found in the 92-year-old millionaire woman's wallet. (This sentence uses definitive, specific, and concrete terms, *One thousand dollars* and *92-year-old millionaire*, to define the rather vague and abstract terms used in the incorrect version.)

The same concept holds true in developing a paragraph. Sentences within the paragraph should remain definitive, specific, concrete, and clear.

> Incorrect: There are many different languages in the world, but English has by far the widest vocabulary. One dictionary lists thousands of English words, and it is estimated that there are several hundred thousand technical and scientific words that have not been cataloged (Ling, 2001). (This paragraph uses vague terms that result in abstract or unclear writing.)
>
> Correct: There are an estimated 2,700 different languages in the world, but English has by far the richest and widest vocabulary. The *Oxford English Dictionary* lists about 500,000 English words, and it is estimated that there are another half-million technical and scientific words that have not been cataloged (Ling, 2001). (This paragraph uses definitive, specific, and concrete terms that result in clear and precise understanding of the writing.)

Avoid useless words

In some cases, writers think that using more words results in better writing. Unfortunately, this is far from the truth. Too many words can become cumbersome and confusing. These useless or unneeded words result in confusion and misinterpretation on the reader's part. So, while on the surface it may appear as though many words create a scholarly writing piece, the reality is these excess words should be eliminated.

Consider the following examples:

This explanation and additional examples further explain Strunk & White's Chapter II (Rule #17).

Useless wording	Use instead
revert back	revert
until such time as	until
end result	result
same identical	same or identical
came at a time when	when
free gift	free or gift

The above examples indicate that using too many words can actually add confusion to writing. Using fewer words often times results in easier comprehension.

Avoid a succession of loose sentences

This explanation and additional examples further explain Strunk & White's Chapter II (Rule #18).

Writing too many consecutive sentences with two clauses (either dependent or independent) along with a connective element can result in awkward writing. A connective element includes a conjunction (*and, but, or, nor, etc.*) or a nonrestrictive word (*which, who, while, etc.*) While the sentences may be grammatically correct, successive writing in this style results in choppy reading and potential misinterpretation. Consider the following paragraph:

> We left for vacation on a cold, dreary, rainy day, even though it was July in northern Michigan. We were extremely excited to be leaving, and the weather didn't dampen our spirits. Eight hours later, we arrived at our destination, Sandusky, Ohio. The weather wasn't much better, but the children were extremely excited to finally arrive at Cedar Point! Upon entering the park, they ran to the roller coaster line. Even though the weather didn't cooperate, the entertainment park proved to be an incredible experience for everyone! We now definitely agree with the old adage: "A rainy day on vacation is better than a sunny day at work!"

The sentences are grammatically correct, but they do not flow logically. When the paragraph is read aloud, it is obvious that there are an inordinate amount of consecutive sentences connected by either a conjunction or nonrestrictive clause. A simple rewrite provides for easier reading:

We left for vacation on a cold, dreary, rainy day. It was July in northern Michigan. We were extremely excited to be leaving, and the weather didn't dampen our spirits. We arrived at our destination (Sandusky, Ohio) eight hours later. Although the weather wasn't much better, the children were extremely excited to finally arrive at Cedar Point! They immediately ran to the roller coaster line. The entertainment park proved to be an incredible experience for everyone! We now definitely agree with the old adage: "A rainy day on vacation is better than a sunny day at work!"

This explanation and additional examples further explain Strunk & White's Chapter II (Rule #18).

Both paragraphs have the same content and meaning. However, the second paragraph flows logically and does not contain excessive pauses due to conjunctions and restrictive words. A prudent author uses a mix of writing to convey concise and clear content.

Expressing coordinate ideas in similar form

Parallel construction

A sentence is considered parallel when related words, phrases, or clauses are placed using a consistent style/structure. When a sentence uses different styles/structures for related words, phrases, or clauses, faulty parallelism results.

Incorrect: Jonathan enjoys hunting with his father, taking long hikes in the woods, and he likes to snowboard with his friends. (*He likes to snowboard with his friends* is not consistent with the other elements in the series.)

Correct: Jonathan enjoys hunting with his father, taking long hikes in the woods, and snowboarding with his friends. (All elements are consistent using *ing*.)

This explanation and additional examples further explain Strunk & White's Chapter II (Rule #19).

Correlative wording

Correlative words and expressions (*not only*, *but also*; *either*, *or*; *neither*, *nor*; *etc.*) must also abide by parallelism. When these types of words or phrases are used in writing, consistency with style and structure is a necessity. Consider the following incorrect and correct examples.

Incorrect: He not only bought the cake, but he ate the entire thing! (incorrect use of *not only*, *but also*)

Correct: He not only bought the cake, but also ate the entire thing! (correct use of *not only*, *but also*)

Incorrect: Either you can attend college or get employment. (incorrect use of *either*, *or*)

Correct: You can either attend college or find employment. (correct use of *either*, *or*)

Incorrect: The dog was neither cute or friendly. (incorrect use of *neither*, *nor*)

Correct: The dog was neither cute nor friendly. (correct use of *neither*, *nor*)

This explanation and additional examples further explain Strunk & White's Chapter II (Rule #20).

Related words

Words and groups of words that are related should be placed together

Placement of words is of utmost importance when writing. Related words need to be positioned next to each other. If not, the end result is reader confusion and misunderstanding.

Misplaced modifiers

A misplaced modifier does not clearly modify, or explain, the intended word. A modifier must be placed directly before the word it is modifying. Consider the following examples:

Incorrect: Walking down the sidewalk, a speeding car sprayed me with dirty water. (The *car*, obviously, was not walking down the street.)

Correct: While I was walking down the street, a speeding car sprayed me with dirty water. (This clearly indicates that *I* was walking down the street.)

Incorrect: The house went up for sale that was burglarized. (*That was burglarized* modifies the house and should be near the word it describes. In this example, the phrase might be misinterpreted as modifying *sale*.)

Correct: The house that was burglarized went up for sale. (*That was burglarized* modifies the house. Therefore, the sentence makes sense when the phrase is placed directly after the word it describes.)

This explanation and additional examples further explain Strunk & White's Chapter II (Rule #20).

Other commonly misplaced modifiers include *only, even,* and *just.*

Misplaced phrases and clauses

Phrases and clauses sometimes may not appear directly before the words that they modify. However, it is imperative that the intended meaning be clearly stated. Otherwise, the sentence results in confusion and misunderstanding.

Incorrect: After being released from prison, the judge ordered the convicted felon to wear a tether for six months. (This phrase implies that the *judge* was released from prison.)

Correct: After being released from prison, the convicted felon was ordered by the judge to wear a tether for six months. (This properly worded sentence correctly indicates that the *convicted felon* was ordered to wear the tether...not the judge.)

Dangling modifiers

Similar to a misplaced phrase or clause, a dangling modifier does not appropriately reference any part of the sentence.

> Incorrect: Deciding to try out for the football team, the coach encouraged the student to elevate his grade point average. (This implies that the *coach* decided to try out for the football team.)
>
> Correct: Deciding to try out for the football team, the student was encouraged by the coach to elevate his grade point average. (This properly worded sentence correctly indicates that the *student* decided to try out for the football team...not the coach.)

Summarizing in one tense

Be consistent with tense when developing a summary

Summaries depend on the type of writing. For example, drama requires the use of present tense, and novels can use either present or past based on writer preference. The critical point is to remain consistent...whichever method is utilized. Various websites exist that pertain to summary writing, so it is suggested to view the different guidelines and requirements when developing a summary.

This explanation and additional examples further explain Strunk & White's Chapter II (Rule #21).

Emphatic word placement

Placing emphatic words toward the end or beginning of the sentence

Emphatic and definite words are generally placed near the end of a sentence. The later placement provides emphasis on the first portion of the sentence and provides an amplification of its meaning.

The other area of placement for emphatic words is the beginning of the sentence. When the subject is preceded by these types of vivid descriptors, the words become more pronounced. The following examples exemplify this concept:

> Nathaniel can't support your viewpoint – he vehemently opposes your position! (*He vehemently opposes your position!* amplifies the importance of the initial portion of the sentence.)
>
> Categorically denying wrongdoing, Chelsea walked off the stand and back to her seat in the courtroom. (*Categorically denying wrongdoing* is placed first to emphasize Chelsea's defense.)

This explanation and additional examples further explain Strunk & White's Chapter II (Rule #22).

Part III: Form

Colloquialism Use

Colloquialisms, known as informal or slang language (*ain't*, *y'all*, *blind as a bat*, *etc.*), should generally be avoided in academic or formal writing. If used, however, do so sparingly and do not draw unneeded emphasis to the word or phrase by setting it off in quotations, italicizing, underlining, or boldfacing the text. Rather, type the word or phrase just as the other text.

Exclamations

Exclamation points are used to emphasize a word or sentence. Do not use an exclamation point to simply complete a sentence. It must clearly indicate emphasis or excitement.

> I knew it would happen! (The exclamation point is placed at the end of the sentence to show emotion.)

Headings

Writing that will be submitted for publication will require specific heading requirements. These requirements are dependent on the publisher. Generally speaking, if the guidelines are not precisely followed, the manuscript will not even be considered for publication. It is strongly recommended, therefore, that writers consult with the publisher prior to submission. This will ensure that the writing is acceptable to be reviewed.

Hyphens

Use hyphens to link compound adjectives (two or more adjectives that modify the same noun) when they precede a noun.

> The heavier-than-air blimp soared over the city. (*Heavier-than-air* is a compound adjective.)
>
> The blue-green dress looked lovely on her. (*Blue-green* is a compound adjective.)

Do not use a hyphen if the compound adjectives follow the actual noun. Additionally, do not use a hyphen with compound adjectives if they are commonly used as phrases that are considered one unit. Finally, do not use a hyphen if the first word of the compound adjective ends in -*ly*.

> The out-of-town visitors left our home in a hurry. (*Out-of-town* is a compound adjective that precedes a noun; therefore, hyphens are required.)
>
> The visitors from out of town left our home in a hurry. (*Out of town* is a compound adjective that follows the noun; therefore, hyphens are not required.)
>
> Most high school students receive their license on their 16th birthday. (*High school* is a commonly used phrase that is considered one unit; therefore, a hyphen is not required.)
>
> The freshly ground coffee smelled delicious. (*Freshly* is an adjective modifying *ground*, which modifies *coffee*. However, *freshly* ends in *ly*; therefore, a hyphen is not required.)

Using hyphens properly can prove to be a very difficult task. Therefore, writers should use hyphens sparingly.

Margins

Margins are generally equally spaced on both the left and right sides. Like with headings, margins requirements may vary when the writing is being considered for publication. Authors should consult with the publisher and submit accordingly.

Numerals

Numbers are an essential part of our language and are used to describe various things such as weights, measurements, ages, times, and quantities. It is important to recognize the difference between a *number,* which is usually spelled out *(thirty seven)* and a *numeral (37),* which is a figure or symbol. Consider the following examples:

Number	Numeral
four	*4*
three hundred	*300*

Below are writing rules that relate specifically to numbers.

Beginning a sentence:

Never begin a sentence with a numeral. In many cases, it is simply easier to modify the sentence so that a number does not appear as the first word.

> Incorrect: *600* people attended the conference.
>
> Correct: There were *600* people in attendance at the conference.
>
> Incorrect: *1,400* people attended the conference.
>
> Correct: *Fourteen hundred* people attended the conference.
>
> Incorrect: *1,000,000* copies of the Michael Jackson album sold during the first month of its release.
>
> Correct: Michael Jackson's album sold over *1,000,000* copies during the first month of its release.

Single-digit numbers:

Single-digit numbers that are less than 10 should be spelled out.

> Incorrect: *4* of *8* dogs made it to the semi-finals in the beauty contest.
>
> Correct: *Four* of *eight* dogs made it to the semi-finals in the beauty contest.
>
> Incorrect: It took *7* years for my neighbor's daughter to finish her bachelor's degree.
>
> Correct: It took *seven* years for my neighbor's daughter to finish her bachelor's degree.

Numbers greater than nine:

Numbers that are greater than nine should be written with numerals. The only exception to this rule, as previously noted, is if the number begins the sentence. Remember, never begin a sentence with a numeral…always spell it out.

> Incorrect: A marathon race is approximately *twenty-six* miles in length.
>
> Correct: A marathon race is approximately *26* miles in length.
>
> Incorrect: There were *eighteen* high school students who tried out for the basketball team, but only *twelve* can actually make the team.
>
> Correct: There were *18* high school students who tried out for the basketball team, but only *12* can actually make the team.

Compound numbers:

Hyphenate all compound numbers from twenty-one through ninety-nine.

Incorrect: *Thirty three* people were leaving on the bus that was headed for Atlanta.

Correct: *Thirty-three* people were leaving on the bus that was headed for Atlanta.

Incorrect: The Boy Scout leader purchased *twenty five* flashlights for the upcoming weekend getaway.

Correct: The Boy Scout leader purchased *twenty-five* flashlights for the upcoming weekend getaway.

Consistency rule with numbers:

When using numbers in writing, consistency is important. When multiple numbers are used within the same sentence, some less than and others over 10, use numerals for all numbers.

Incorrect: The debate team was comprised of *six* Juniors and *12* Seniors.

Correct: The debate team was comprised of *6* Juniors and *12* Seniors.

Incorrect: Marian worked *four* hours on Friday, *10* hours on Saturday, and *12* hours on Sunday.

Correct: Marian worked *4* hours on Friday, *10* hours on Saturday, and *12* hours on Sunday.

Fractions and decimal points:

Simple fractions are always spelled out with a hyphen separating the numerator and denominator.

Incorrect: Speckles, our dog, jumped on the counter and ate *1/2* of the birthday cake.

Correct: Speckles, our dog, jumped on the counter and ate *one-half* of the birthday cake.

Incorrect: Only *1/10* of the senior class decided not to pursue their education.

Correct: Only *one-tenth* of the senior class decided not to pursue their education.

Mixed fractions are expressed in numerals.

Incorrect: The recipe included *two and one-half* cups of sugar.

Correct: The recipe included *2 1/2* cups of sugar.

A comma is used with numbers that have decimal points only when the number has four or more digits to the left of the decimal point. The comma should be placed in front of the third digit to the left of the decimal point.

Incorrect: He spent *eight thousand, twenty-six dollars and twenty-two cents*.

Correct: He spent *$8,026.22*.

Decades:

Specific decades should be spelled out in lowercase letters.

> Incorrect: My favorite music was produced in the *Seventies* and *Eighties*.
>
> Correct: My favorite music was produced in the *seventies* and *eighties*.
>
> Incorrect: Some people will argue that the United States suffered a recession in the *Nineties.*
>
> Correct: Some people will argue that the United States suffered a recession in the *nineties.*

Decades can also be expressed using numerals. When this is done, there is no apostrophe between the numerals and the *s.*

> Incorrect: The *1700's* and *1800's* were periods of great change in architecture.
>
> Correct: The *1700s* and *1800s* were periods of great change in architecture.
>
> Incorrect: Gangsters ruled Chicago in the *1920's.*
>
> Correct: Gangsters ruled Chicago in the *1920s.*

Dates and time of day:

The time of day can be either spelled out or indicated by numerals. If the term *o'clock* is used, the time must be spelled out. When a sentence includes a month and day, simply give the day as a numeral. When referring to specific day dates within a sentence, use *st*, *nd*, *th*, or *rd* as needed (*e.g., first, second, fifth, third*).

> Incorrect: Starting work at *5:00 o'clock* is very difficult.
>
> Correct: Starting work at *five o'clock* is very difficult.
>
> Incorrect: The conference will end on *January 13th*.
>
> Correct: The conference will end on *January 13*.
>
> Incorrect: February *23rd* is Tiffany's birthday.
>
> Correct: February *23* is Tiffany's birthday.
>
> Incorrect: I will receive my Social Security check on the *23* of each month.
>
> Correct: I will receive my Social Security check on the *23rd* of each month.

Parentheses

Parentheses are used much like dashes to add information. The difference between parentheses and dashes is that parentheses de-emphasize the information they enclose while dashes emphasize the information that follows. Parentheses are always used in pairs.

> We're going to dinner (date night); however, I'll see you in the morning. (*Date night* is set off in parentheses because it is not a necessary part of the sentence.)
>
> You are always here for me — you are my very best friend! (*You are my very best friend* emphasizes the importance of the first part of the sentence and is therefore set off with a dash.)

Quotations

Quotation marks are used to indicate the exact words of a source, either written or spoken. They are generally used in pairs, with one set of quotation marks used at the beginning of the direct quotation, and a second set used at the end of the direct quotation. Single quotation marks are used only to replace any double quotation marks that appear in the original quotation.

Short direct quotations

Direct quotations are exact words spoken by someone other than the writer. A quotation is used to enhance the writer's viewpoint. The entire quotation is placed within quotation marks.

"It's all in how you choose to look at it," Dr. Connie Harrison so eloquently explained. (*It's all in how you choose to look at it* is a direct quotation and is set off within quotation marks.)   William Arthur Ward stated, "The mediocre teacher tells. The good teacher explains. The superior teacher demonstrates. The great teacher inspires." (The entire direct quotation is placed within quotation marks.)

Indirect quotations not requiring quotation marks

An indirect quotation is when the writer paraphrases another source. These types of quotations are not enclosed in quotation marks.

The company representative said that the CEO had left the firm. (Since this is an indirect quotation, no quotation marks are needed.)

Long direct quotations

Long quotations, generally four or more typed lines, are indented one inch from the left margin. No quotation marks are required, as the indentation implies a direct quotation.

Mother Theresa was famous for the following quotation:

Life is an opportunity, benefit from it.

Life is beauty, admire it.

Life is bliss, taste it.

Life is a dream, realize it.

Life is a challenge, meet it.

Life is a duty, complete it.

Life is a game, play it.

Life is a promise, fulfill it.

Life is sorrow, overcome it.

Life is a song, sing it.

Life is a struggle, accept it.

Life is a tragedy, confront it.

Life is an adventure, dare it.

Life is luck, make it.

Life is too precious, do not destroy it.

Life is life, fight for it.

Steve Jobs provides another example of a long quotation:

Your time is limited; don't waste it living someone else's life. Don't be trapped by dogma, which is living the result of other people's thinking. Don't let the noise of another's opinion drown your own inner voice. And most important, have the courage to follow your heart and intuition; they somehow already know what you truly want to become. Everything else is secondary.

Using Single Quotation Marks

Use single quotation marks to set off a quotation that is placed within a quotation.

> George said, "I'm not really 'afraid.' I'm just cautious."
> (*Afraid* is a quotation within a quotation. Therefore, it is enclosed with only single quotation marks.)

References

Scholarly writing will undoubtedly include references listed throughout the work. There are multiple writing style formats that indicate ways in which to cite references… both within the actual text and the ending reference/ bibliography page. The writer must select a style and adhere to those specific guidelines. One rule applies to all writing styles: Always provide appropriate credit; otherwise, it is considered plagiarism!

Syllabication (word division)

When a word requires a division (using a hyphen) at the end of a line, the division must occur between syllables. All syllables will have one vowel sound. Therefore, the number of vowel sounds will equate to the number of syllables.

> The word *syllabication* has five syllables (*syl-lab-i-ca-tion*).
>
> It can be divided at any point in the syllable break *syl-lab-i-ca-tion*.

Do not hyphenate one syllable words or extremely short words. Additionally, the word that is being divided must have at least three letters on the first line. Likewise, "carried over letters" – those that appear on the second line – must include three or more letters. When in doubt, consult a dictionary for proper division.

Part IV:
Commonly Misused Words

This section refers to section IV of Strunk & White's book titled *Words and Expressions Commonly Misused*.

Below are words that can be used to prevent careless, vague, or improper writing. These words exceed those noted by Strunk & White so writers get a better understanding of the subject matter.

A

Abdicate – relinquish, resign. Jeannie will not abdicate her position.

Abhorrent – loathsome, offensive. The old log cabin was abhorrent.

Acumen – insight, smart. Rachelle wants to improve her business acumen.

Adjourn – suspend, postpone. The judge decided to adjourn for the day.

Affidavit – sworn statement, deposition. John's statement was viewed as an affidavit.

Aghast – horrified, shocked. Rachael was aghast when she saw the body.

Albatross – impediment, burden. His old dog was starting to become an albatross.

Along the lines – like, comparable. Avoid using due to excessive wordiness.

> Incorrect: Terrance is studying along the lines of classic literature.
>
> Correct: Terrance is studying classic literature.

Alternate – every other, one of two, not the same as *alternative*. Cecil chose an alternate route to the castle because he had no alternative.

Ambiguous – equivocal, vague. Randell thought the clue was ambiguous.

Amelioration – improvement, editing. His book needs amelioration.

Anachronistic – outdated, antiquated. His tie was anachronistic.

Anomalous – irregular, inconstant. Her testimony was anomalous.

Anybody – any person, any group. Cannot be written as two words. Has anybody seen Roger?

Anyone – one person, one thing. Cannot be written as two words. Does anyone understand the question?

Aphrodisiac – sexual, erotic. The new drug functions as an aphrodisiac.

Apocryphal – fictional, fake. The monster story is apocryphal.

Apprehension – pause, seizure. Brett felt apprehension when pressed to get married.

Arrayed – displayed, arranged. The lamb chops were arrayed in a glass case on the butcher shop counter.

Aspire – strive, seek. Nicky does not aspire to be an actress.

Assiduous – diligent, careful. Zebras are assiduous about their feeding grounds.

As of yet – remove *as of*.

Incorrect: She has not made the team as of yet.
Correct: She has not made the team yet.

As to whether – remove *as to*.

Incorrect: He had to decide as to whether or not to play baseball.
Correct: He had to decide whether or not to play baseball.

Atone – apologize, beg pardon. Mandy wants to atone for her poor choice of words.

Austere – harsh, severe. They hiked a trail with austere terrain.

Averse – disinclined, opposed. Thomas was averse to the move.

B

Balk – refuse, hesitate. He knew she would balk at his proposal.

Befuddle – confuse, baffle. Her actions appeared to befuddle him.

Being – existing, person. Do not use after *regarded as*.

Incorrect: Norma is regarded as being the best teacher.
Correct: Norma is regarded as the best teacher.

Belated – late, delayed. D'Andre wished her a belated happy birthday.

Blatant – flagrant, obvious. Bob's foul on the opposing player was blatant.

Brash – pushy, brazen. She is a brash person.

Buoyant – floatable, afloat. The boat was buoyant throughout the voyage.

But – although, however.

> Incorrect: Gina had no doubt but that she was thrown under the bus by George.
>
> Correct: Gina had no doubt that she was thrown under the bus by George.
>
> Incorrect: Gina could not help but be offended by George's comment.
>
> Correct: Gina could not help being offended by George's comment.

Buttressed – bolstered, supported. The support buttressed the wall.

C

Cajole – coax, persuade. Helen tried to cajole Wayne into giving her his keys.

Calamity – disaster, tragedy. The damaged bridge is a calamity.

Callous – hardened, heartless. Mindy is a callous person.

Can – am able, know how. I can play the piano. Do not confuse with *may*.

> Incorrect: Can I go to the restroom?
>
> Correct: May I go to the restroom?

Capitulate – surrender, submit. The red team planned to capitulate at dawn.

Capricious – fickle, unpredictable. Jessabelle is a very capricious person.

Case – situation, circumstance. This word is often not
    necessary.

> Incorrect: In almost every case, the athletes could not
> complete the course.
>
> Correct: Almost all of the athletes could not complete the
> course.

Castigate – criticize, reprimand. Please do not castigate me
    in front of my boss.

Character – person, individual. Avoid using for wordiness
    reasons.

> Incorrect: The actions of a mean character caused the
> hatred.
>
> Correct: Mean actions caused the hatred.

Clandestine – covert, secret. His role in the sting is
    clandestine.

Clemency – compassion, mercy. The judge gave clemency to
    the defendant.

Congeal – solidify, coagulate. The substance will congeal at
    low temperatures.

Consider – ponder, contemplate. Do not use *as* after this
    word when it means *believe it to be*. Use *as* after this
    work when it means *examined*. I consider Normandy first
    as a city, second as a battleground, and third as a symbol
    of freedom.

> Incorrect: I consider Jill as honest.
>
> Correct: I consider Jill honest.

Conspicuous – noticeable, visible. The tattoo on Linda's arm
    is conspicuous.

Cope – manage, handle. People do not cope; they cope with a person, place, or thing.

> Incorrect: I knew he could cope.
>
> Correct: I knew he could cope with her behavior.

Covenant – agreement, pact. The covenant states that dogs are not allowed on the premises.

Currently – now, presently. Avoid redundancy when it is not necessary.

> Incorrect: We are currently living in Alaska.
>
> Correct: We are living in Alaska.

D

Dastardly – shameful, dishonorable. Tony is a dastardly man.

Deft – skilled, adroit. Maryanne is a deft individual.

Delude – deceive, cheat. Jenny was able to delude Keonte about the real meaning of the story.

Demented – insane, crazy. Roger is a demented individual.

Denigrate – belittle, ridicule. Please do not denigrate my brother.

Deposition – statement, testimony. Kerry gave her deposition to the judge.

Depot – storehouse, warehouse. The groceries are at the Milwaukee depot.

Despondent – hopeless, dejected. Valerie was despondent over her husband's termination.

Different than – use sparingly if other wording is more logical.

> Incorrect: All stars are different than each other.
>
> Correct: All stars differ from each other.

Dilute – watery, thinned. Pam forgot to dilute her laundry soap.

Discern – notice, detect. Rafael could not discern any problems with the car he rented.

Disheveled – rumpled, unkempt. Jeremy looked tired and disheveled.

Dissuade – persuade against, discourage. Monica tried to dissuade her boyfriend from going into the military.

Divided into – split up, separated. Do not confuse with *composed of*. Plays are divided into acts, and albums are composed of songs.

Dubious – doubtful, uncertain. Erica's position seemed dubious after her review.

Due to – owing to, as a result of. Use for *attributed to* rather than *because of*. She lost her lunch because of her carelessness, but the picnic was canceled due to bad weather.

E

Ebullient – enthusiastic, jovial. Orville was ebullient about his engagement to Dolores.

Edify – educate, inform. Anita always tries to edify non-believers about Jesus Christ.

Effect – result, outcome. Do not confuse with *affect*. The weather had a damaging effect on the house, but the weather did not affect the barn.

Eloquent – articulate, expressive. Mike's sermon was eloquent.

Emaciated – gaunt, wasted. Yolanda was emaciated after the marathon.

Enormity – horror, wickedness. Do not use to express something that is large or huge. Calvin was shocked by the enormity of the accident, but a huge burden was lifted when he learned that it was not his fault.

Epitaph – inscription, caption. David wants "He was a good man" as an epitaph on his gravestone.

Epitome – essence, embodiment. Rex was the epitome of a good dog.

Eradicate – eliminate, destroy. Mary wanted the pest control company to eradicate the mice in her house.

Erratic – inconsistent, irregular. Donald's behavior was erratic.

Espouse – adopt, support. Melissa would not espouse her brother's business idea.

Etc. – so forth, and the rest. Do not drink sweetened beverages such as energy drinks, soda, chocolate milk, *etc.* Do not use in place of *et al.* for authors.

Incorrect: Johnson, Smith, Barley, *etc.*

Correct: Johnson, Smith, Barley, *et al.*

Excoriate – attack, criticize. Please do not excoriate my training program.

Exhilarate – invigorate, excite. You will exhilarate Jan if you buy her a new car.

Extricate – remove, extract. John tried to extricate the sliver from his finger.

Exultant – joyful, jubilant. Katie was exultant over her promotion.

F

Facility – building, structure. The manufacturing facility is at the end of the street. A hospital, school, or jail should not be called a *facility*.

> Incorrect: She attended class at the facility.
>
> Correct: She attended class at the university.

Fact – happening, occurrence. It is a fact that air contains oxygen. Do not use if it cannot be verified.

> Incorrect: It is a fact that Richard Nixon was the greatest president in the history of the United States.
>
> Correct: It is believed by some people that Richard Nixon was the greatest president in the history of the United States.

Factor – aspect, feature. Timing is a factor. Use sparingly by replacing with wording that is more direct.

> Incorrect: Strategy was the determining factor for him winning the race.
>
> Correct: He won the race with strategy.

Farce – sham, absurd. The treasure map is a farce.

Farther – beyond, past. Do not confuse with *further.* Isadore went farther in the Spanish program than anyone else, and now he plans to further his education in a different language.

Feature – characteristic, trait. Leather seats are a feature. Use sparingly by replacing with wording that is more direct.

> Incorrect: One feature of the play that deserves to be mentioned is the final scene.
>
> Correct: The final scene of the play deserves to be mentioned.

Feeble – weak, frail. His sickness made him feeble.

Fidelity – faithfulness, loyalty. Fidelity is important for a good marriage.

Filial – loving, devoted. Jessie has a filial affection for his aunt.

Flammable – combustible, incendiary. This word has the same meaning as *inflammable*, but the *in* prevents many people from understanding.

Incorrect: The firefighter's socks were inflammable.
Correct: The firefighter's socks were flammable.

Folk – society, people. Do not use the plural form *folks*, and do not use in formal writing when referring to parents.

Incorrect: Mario went to see his folks.
Correct: Mario went to see his mother and father.
Incorrect: Rafael likes the folks from his home town.
Correct: Rafael likes the folk from his hometown.

Fortuitous – chance, accidental. Do not confuse with *fortunate*. Rosie was fortuitous when she stumbled upon the lawn mower in the old barn, and she was fortunate that it started on the first pull.

Frivolous – trivial, silly. The lawsuit was deemed frivolous.

Fulminate – rant, rage. The cashiers continued to fulminate over their pay cuts.

Futile – vain, trivial. Jackie's effort was futile.

G

Gale – storm, gust. The winds were gale force.

Galvanized – electrified, roused. Cindy was happy that she galvanized Gerry into taking immediate action.

Gauche – clumsy, awkward. Veronica is a gauche person.

Genial – friendly, warm. Penelope has a genial personality.

Grandeur – magnificence, splendor. They are restoring the church to its original grandeur.

Gravity – severity, importance. The gravity of his actions is not known.

Grotesque – hideous, ugly. The half-eaten deer was grotesque.

H

Harangue – tirade, scolding. Michael delivered a harangue about his dissatisfaction with his teacher.

He is a man who – avoid redundancy of this phrase and similar wording.

Incorrect: He is a man who likes to gamble.
Correct: He likes to gamble.
Incorrect: Brazil is a country that never experiences snow.
Correct: Brazil never experiences snow.

Hegemony – domination, control. Poland was under German hegemony during the Second World War.

Heinous – atrocious, terrible. Her actions were truly heinous.

Heresy – dissenting, deviation. The politician was burned at the stake for heresy.

Hue – type, shade. The ocean water has a deep blue hue.

I

Impeach – accuse, prosecute. The committee voted to impeach the president.

Impetuous – impulsive, hasty. Impetuous young people have been known to join the military.

Importantly – significant, prominent. Try to refrain from using this word and always avoid overusing it.

> Incorrect: More importantly, she was not at her job.
>
> Correct: More important, she was not at her job.

Importunate – unrelenting, persistent. Erin was importunate in her quest for a better grade.

In terms of – avoid using this phrase in writing.

> Incorrect: Her move to Oregon was a mistake in terms of happiness.
>
> Correct: Her unhappiness made the move to Oregon a mistake.

Inadvertent – unintentional, negligent. Her actions were inadvertent, but they were still damaging.

Incensed – angry, enraged. Rocco was incensed over his termination.

Incongruous – odd, strange. Rita appeared incongruous as she sat in the corner.

Indignation – outrage, resentment. Harold experienced indignation when he was asked to leave the building.

Infamous – disreputable, wicked. Do not confuse with *famous*. Elvis Presley was famous, and Charles Manson was infamous.

Infatuation – crush, obsession. Nancy has an infatuation with red flowers.

Innate – inborn, native. Rhonda has an innate ability to jump high.

Innuendo – inference, allusion. Jim's innuendo upset his father.

Inside of – inside, within. Eliminate the word *of.*

> Incorrect: Catelyn peeked inside of the store.
>
> Correct: Catelyn peeked inside the store.

Integral – fundamental, essential. A chain is an integral part of a bike.

Intent – focused, determined. Wally's intent was not to hurt the other player.

Irregardless – Unrelatedly, irrespective. Use *regardless* as a replacement.

> Incorrect: Irregardless of her fear, she made the change.
>
> Correct: Regardless of her fear, she made the change.

–ize – suffix. Avoid using *ize* if it is unnecessary.

> Incorrect: Utilize the dictionary as needed.
>
> Correct: Use the dictionary as needed.

J

Jaunty – jolly, cheerful. Rebecca's friend is polite and jaunty.

Jocular – humorous, funny. Rebecca's friend is also jocular.

K

Kaleidoscopic – complex, colorful. The landscape had a kaleidoscopic appearance.

Kind of – similar to, rather. Axel appeared kind of sad. Do not use in place of *something like.*

> Incorrect: A gerbil looks kind of like a mouse.
>
> Correct: A gerbil looks something like a mouse.

L

Languish – suffer, weaken. Harvey did not want his dog to languish and agonize.

Laudable – commendable, credible. Tom is a laudable human being.

Lay – rest, place. Do not confuse with *lie*. A chicken will lay an egg, and a goat will lie down.

Let – allow, permit. Do not confuse with *leave*.

Incorrect: Leave it go until tomorrow.
Correct: Let it go until tomorrow.

Liaison – link, connection. Bernie is the company's liaison to the government.

Like – resembles, similar. It looks like a rainbow. Do not use in place of *as*.

Incorrect: We walked down to the lake like we did in the past.
Correct: We walked down to the lake as we did in the past.

Livid – furious, angry. Donna was livid over the change in direction.

Loan – borrow, advance. Pamela considered the money a loan. Use *lend* as a replacement.

Incorrect: Rolando is going to loan Peter the money.
Correct: Rolando is going to lend Peter the money.

Lucid – bright, clear. Karen's explanation was lucid.

Ludicrous – ridiculous, absurd. Xavier's proposal was ludicrous.

M

Malevolent – malicious, spiteful. His actions were malevolent.

Mandate – command, order. The rule is a mandate rather than a suggestion.

Melancholy – sad, pensive. Dennis is a melancholy man.

Memento – reminder, souvenir. Do not confuse with *momento*.

Incorrect: Jillian kept the seashell as a momento of her trip.
Correct: Jillian kept the seashell as a memento of her trip.

Meticulous – careful, exact. My son's room is meticulous.

Mitigate – alleviate, soften. Jerome failed to mitigate the problem when telling his brother.

Moot – controversial, disputable. Don't confuse with *mute*.

Incorrect: Your opinion is a mute point.
Correct: Your opinion is a moot point.

Most – mainly, largely. Most people prefer printed versions of books. Replace with *almost* in formal writing.

Incorrect: Johnson and Smith did most all of the research.
Correct: Johnson and Smith did almost all of the research.

N

Nature – class, kind. Avoid using for redundancy.

Incorrect: Her office job is of a sedentary nature.
Correct: Her office job is sedentary.

Nauseous – sickened, disgusted. Do not confuse with *nauseated*. Annette found the waiter's appearance nauseous and felt nauseated after eating the dinner he served her.

Nebulous – vague, hazy. Her description of her house was quite nebulous.

Nemesis – opponent, enemy. Ernie was Orlando's arch nemesis.

Nirvana – paradise, bliss. Andrea's happiness put her in a state of nirvana.

Nondescript – uninteresting, ordinary. The painting was nondescript.

Notoriety – Infamy, dishonor. Her notoriety worked against her in court.

Null – valueless, worthless. The contract was null and void.

O

Obdurate – unyielding, stubborn. Sally is an obdurate person.

Obtrude – interfere, meddle. Please do not obtrude in my business.

Ominous – doomed, warning. The deserted town was very ominous.

One – single, solitary. Do not follow with *him* or *her*.

Incorrect: One must be aware of his actions.
Correct: One must be aware of one's actions.

Onerous – burdensome, tiresome. Melody completed an onerous task.

Orator – speaker, lecturer. Ted is a great orator.

Ordination – conferment, consecration. All of the priests went through the ordination ceremony.

Oriented – positioned, based. Avoid using this term when defining alignment, placement, direction, or position.

> Incorrect: The company is very production-oriented.
>
> Correct: The company is mainly concerned with production.

P

Partially – do not confuse with *partly*. I am partially committed to the club because I am partly in and partly out.

Pathos – despair, sadness. The pathos of the situation numbed Angela's senses.

Perfidious – dishonest, deceitful. Anthony is always involved in perfidious activities.

Perfunctorily – routinely, automatically. Daniella wakes up every morning perfunctorily.

Personally – individually, for myself. This word is not necessary in most writing.

> Incorrect: Personally, I was pleased by his offer.
>
> Correct: I was pleased by his offer.

Perturbation – worry, alarm. Tara experienced little perturbation about her safety.

Pestilent – lethal, deadly. Rattlesnake bites have the potential to be pestilent.

Pinnacle – highpoint, peak. Myra reached the pinnacle of her career.

Placid – easygoing, mild. Marco is a very placid person.

Plausible – reasonable, believable. Barry's solution appeared to be plausible.

Postulate – assume, guess. We can only postulate that Ingrid chose the best route.

Prerogative – right, entitlement. Smoking is your prerogative.

Presently – soon, now. This word is confusing because it has two meanings, so restrict its use to *soon*.

> Incorrect: Terry will be here soon, but presently she is at the ranch.
>
> Correct: Terry will be here presently, but now she is at the ranch.

Pugnacious – belligerent, aggressive. I wish Eleanor was not so pugnacious.

Q

Quagmire – swamp, marsh. Queenie had difficulty navigating through the quagmire.

Querulous – difficult, complaining. Angel is a querulous person.

Quiescent – calm, inactive. Howard was glad that the fight was over and everything was quiescent.

R

Rapacious – greedy, grasping. It is obvious that Jaqueline is a rapacious woman.

Rebuke – censure, reprimand. Jodie decided to rebuke the accountant for his mistakes.

Recompense – payment, reparation. Fred's real recompense was his freedom.

Regretful – remorseful, sorry. Do not confuse with *regrettable*.

> Incorrect: The problem was due to a regrettable argument.
>
> Correct: The problem was due to a regretful argument.

Relate – tell, recount. He began to relate the details to the detective. Do not use to suggest rapport.

> Incorrect: Phil could not relate to Bernie.
>
> Correct: Phil and Bernie have different viewpoints.

Respective – particular, corresponding. Omit *respective* and *respectively* in most writing.

> Incorrect: Each runner started in his respective lane, and the race was won by Mick and Keith respectively.
>
> Correct: Each runner started in his lane, and Mick won the race with Keith finishing second.

Reticence – reserve, shyness. Pernell's reticence was obvious at the luncheon.

Rhetoric – oratory, speech. Larry's rhetoric was the main reason Theo signed the document.

Ruminate – ponder, reflect. Gayle needs to ruminate on the facts before making any major decision.

S

Salient – important, prominent. Job losses were a salient part of the union lawsuit.

Secular – worldly, nonspiritual. Jackson lives a secular life.

So – subsequently, consequently. Nelly was sad, so she cried. Avoid using to intensify.

> Incorrect: The water was so cold.
>
> Correct: The water was very cold.

Sonorous – resonant, loud. His voice is extremely sonorous.

Spurious – false, bogus. Sanford made a spurious accusation.

Student body – educational group, educational gathering. Omit this phrase most of the time because it is not needed.

> Incorrect: Delores would like to become a member of the student body.
>
> Correct: Delores would like to become a student.

Subterfuge – ploy, deceit. Linda uses subterfuge to get people to agree with her.

Superfluous – excessive, extra. The teacher gave the class a superfluous amount of homework.

Surreptitious – secret, sneaky. His actions at night are somewhat surreptitious.

T

Taunt – insult, ridicule. Do not confuse with *taut*.

> Incorrect: Willie began to taut his adversary.
>
> Correct: Willie began to taunt his adversary.

Tenuous – weak, fragile. Edward's condition was tenuous.

Tepid – lukewarm, indifferent. Malinda's reception of her guests was tepid.

The foreseeable future – ahead, near. Do not use this phrase because it is nondescript and vague.

> Incorrect: In the foreseeable future, Valerie will take her bird to the veterinarian.
>
> Correct: Valerie will take her bird to the veterinarian by Friday.

The truth is – fact, real. Do not use this phrase at the beginning of a sentence.

> Incorrect: The truth is, Reginald wants to marry Regina.
>
> Correct: Reginald wants to marry Regina.

They – individuals, people. Do not use to describe a single person.

> Incorrect: Every member of the team, regardless of whether they played in the game, is unhappy with the loss.
>
> Correct: Every member of the team, regardless of whether he played in the game, is unhappy with the loss.

This – it, that. This store closes at noon. Do not use when other words provide a better description.

> Incorrect: She did a lot of research for her paper, and this shows that she wants to succeed.
>
> Correct: She did a lot of research for her paper, and her effort shows that she wants to succeed.

Throng – crowd, multitude. A throng of people gathered to see the magician.

Tortuous – twisting, winding. Do not confuse with *torturous*.

> Incorrect: The road was torturous at every turn.
>
> Correct: The road was tortuous at every turn.

Truncated – shortened, condensed. The elephant's tusks were truncated after the attack.

Try – attempt, stab. Do not insert *and* after the word, insert *to* instead.

> Incorrect: Helen will try and walk the entire path.
>
> Correct: Helen will try to walk the entire path.

Turbulent – blustery, raging. Kendall documented the turbulent wind in her diary.

U

Ubiquitous – abundant, omnipresent. The seaweed in the lake was ubiquitous.

Unanimous – agreed, unified. The vote was unanimous.

Unique – exceptional, single. There are no degrees of this word.

Incorrect: The vase was very unique.
Correct: The vase was unique.

Usurp – seize, take. Richard was known to usurp power in virtually every situation.

Utilize – use, apply. Avoid using this word. Choose *use* as a replacement.

Incorrect: I need to utilize the hammer.
Correct: I need to use the hammer.

V

Vehemently – fervently, zealously. Louie vehemently denied taking the computer.

Verbal – vocal, voiced. Do not use when the wording is not verbatim.

Incorrect: His verbal response was that he did not care about the raccoon's life.
Correct: His verbal response was, "I am not concerned about the raccoon's life."

Very – actual, appropriate. Use this word sparingly to avoid over emphasizing.

Incorrect: Xavier is very happy with his job.
Correct: Xavier is happy with his job.

Vigorous – powerful, dynamic. She gave the soda a vigorous shake with both hands.

Vile – disgusting, repulsive. Nathan is a vile human being.

Vivacity – liveliness, animation. The vivacity of the event captivated the audience.

W

While – whereas, however. Veronica enjoyed the movie while her husband thought it was boring.

-wise – about, as for. Use sparingly at the end of a word.

Incorrect: He was discontent marriagewise.
Correct: He was discontent with his marriage.

Worthwhile – useful, valuable. Mario wants his effort to be worthwhile instead of wasted. Avoid using this word when it is for approval or disapproval.

Incorrect: The band is not worthwhile.
Correct: The band is not worth watching.

Would – did, will. Avoid using this word if it is not necessary.

Incorrect: She would walk to school every day.
Correct: he walked to school every day.

X

Xerox – photo, replication. Use *copy* as a replacement.

Incorrect: Jan is going to Xerox the document.
Correct: Jan is going to copy the document.

Y

Yield – surrender, defer. Rachael was forced to yield to the pedestrian.

Z

Zealous – enthusiastic, fervid. Marianne has a zealous personality.

Zenith – summit, peak. Francine reached the zenith of the mountain.

Part V:
Individual Writing Styles

This chapter explores individual writing styles and the meaning of the written words. In short, it assesses the spirit of writers and the ways in which their thoughts are revealed to readers. For example, the sentences below have the same meaning, but they are written differently due to individual preference.

> Situations like these are challenging for conservatives.
>
> How challenging are these situations for conservatives!
>
> These situations are challenging for conservatives.

The above sentences express the same thinking, but they are written differently in terms of style. Writers' words highlight the emotions they want to convey to readers. This type of exposure makes it difficult for writers to remain anonymous when they submit or publish work on a regular basis. Consider the impact of the following sentences:

> The forest was part of the nature that was innate to it.
>
> The forest encompassed the nature that was innate to it.
>
> The forest thrived on the nature that was innate to it.

Notice how the forest discussed above progressively comes alive with each sentence. This awakening shows emotion that the writer believes the reader needs for better understanding.

Writing is a labor intensive task that requires time and effort to properly complete. It takes much longer to write words than it does to read them, even though the writing process has been sped up due to modern technology. This time factor has made patience a requirement for writers as they process their thoughts into words. The following are some suggestions for improving writing style while remaining patient:

This explanation and example explain Strunk & White's Chapter V (Rule #1).

Let style emerge by remaining behind the scenes

A careful writer is not concerned with personal style. This statement might seem contradictory because style defines an author, but it is good advice because a reader examines a writing piece as a whole. The work should be written in a way that gets the reader to pay attention to the content, not the author's feelings or temperament. The mood of the writer will gradually appear if the writing is good, and this will be accomplished without affecting the quality of the work. Writers who remain behind the scenes find it easier to break through the obstructions that separate their thoughts from their readers' comprehension of the written material.

> Incorrect: I am completely offended by this change because I am not Catholic and have absolutely no intention of converting.
>
> Correct: People who are not Catholic might be upset by this change.

This explanation and example explain Strunk & White's Chapter V (Rule #2).

Do not force writing style

Good writers allow their words to flow naturally without trying to copy someone else's style. Imitation will inevitably occur, but that occurrence should be the result of an unconscious rather than conscious effort. Words and phrases should come from language that the writer understands and uses on a regular basis so the finished work is truly reflective.

> Incorrect: The decadent, psychologically unappealing structure he was witness to produced an exhilarating epiphany about how to alter society's perception of residential dwellings in urban landscapes.
>
> Correct: The ugly building gave him an idea about how to change people's views of urban housing.

Have a roadmap in place

A roadmap functions as a design that incorporates structure into the writing. It does not have to be as closely followed as a blueprint, but it does need to provide direction. This direction can come from something as simple as a list that gets checked off as the work progresses or it can involve a procedural approach. The idea is to provide a roadmap that helps people avoid the pitfalls of writing without any direction.

This explanation and skeleton explain Strunk & White's Chapter V (Rule #3).

It is important to understand that caution should be exercised when using a roadmap. Some writing does not call for direction because it comes from the heart and soul of a person. A love letter is an example of this type of writing. These letters are usually emotional and spontaneous and structure impedes the process. In most cases, however, there needs to be a skeleton to expand upon, and a roadmap works well as that skeleton.

Consider the following five-part skeleton:

1. *Topic*—Grass cutting technology is the topic.

2. *Introduction*—Introduce grass cutting and tell why it is necessary.

3. *Discussion*—Discuss advantages and disadvantages of different types of grass cutting technology including electric, cordless, gas, mulching, rider, driverless, and push mowers.

4. *Recommendation*—Recommend driverless lawn mowers as the best option and offer support for this recommendation.

5. *Summary*—Summarize by discussing grass cutting and telling why driverless lawn mowers work best.

Use nouns and verbs

This explanation and example explain Strunk & White's Chapter V (Rule #4).

Adverbs and adjectives are a necessary part of the English language because they help writers' express meaning. They cannot, however, replace nouns and verbs. The thinking behind this is simple. Adjectives and adverbs are not as essential as nouns and verbs because they do not add as much strength to a writer's work.

> Incorrect: Rashaad really feels unhappy about his highly competitive nature.
>
> Correct: Rashaad feels unhappy about his competitive nature.

Rework and reprocess

This explanation and example explain Strunk & White's Chapter V (Rule #5).

For writing to be at its best, it needs to be reworked and reprocessed. Writers who examine their work will find mistakes and ways to improve their writing. Flaws will come to the surface, and the work can then be rewritten. Remember that reworking and reprocessing does not indicate weakness or a reason to quit. Instead, it shows a willingness to improve and become a better writer.

> Incorrect: The chare is good as a lumbar support for everyone's lower backs.
>
> Correct: The chair functions well as a lumbar support.

Avoid overwriting

This explanation and example explain Strunk & White's Chapter V (Rule #6).

Writers who step outside of their natural style often end up overwriting. They attempt to make their writing stand out by adding content or substituting easily understood words with those that are more decorative and complex. Overwriting should always be avoided because it has the potential to distort the meaning of a writer's work.

> Incorrect: Janet took a leave of absence similar to a sabbatical so she could categorically complete her work that was of a salient nature.
>
> Correct: Janet took a leave of absence so she could complete her work.

Avoid overstating

Writers who overstate risk losing their readers because those readers lose confidence that the writers will make good judgments. Overstatements are one of the most common types of mistakes made by writers, and one overstatement can distort the entire meaning of the piece. The potential for this problem is ever-present, so writers need to be on guard to avoid sabotaging their work.

This explanation and example explain Strunk & White's Chapter V (Rule #7).

> Incorrect: Everyone hates yellow appliances.
>
> Correct: Many people dislike yellow appliances.

Do not use qualifiers

Little, big, rather, quite, very, and *extremely* are all examples of qualifiers that usurp power from the words that they are describing. Qualifiers are used to assign a quality to a different word, usually a noun, but they serve no real purpose other than to draw attention to themselves. For example, the word *big* should only be used to refer to size, not to emphasize another word because it takes away from that word.

This explanation and example explain Strunk & White's Chapter V (Rule #8).

> Incorrect: The big man created a big catastrophic situation.
>
> Correct: The big man created a catastrophic situation.

Write in a concise and compact manner

This explanation and example explain Strunk & White's Chapter V (Rule #9).

Writers destroy their work when they try to document all of their thoughts with no regard to the effects they have on their readers. If those thoughts are not important or pertinent, then they should not be written. Many writers fail to maintain control of their work, and they end up confusing or losing their readers.

> Incorrect: He walked out the door, while his wife was in the kitchen baking bread in a hot oven and his dog played with a ball, and was never seen again.
>
> Correct: He walked out the door and was never seen again.

Spell words traditionally

This explanation and example explain Strunk & White's Chapter V (Rule #10).

Words should be spelled traditionally because this is the easiest way for them to be understood by readers. For example, the word *lite* might be used to describe a low-calorie soda, but it should not be used when referring to weight. Unless the written work is an introduction to a new type of spelling, stick to the traditional method understood by most people.

> Incorrect: Her dog was lite and easy to carry.
>
> Correct: Her dog was light and easy to carry.

Avoid excessive explanation

This explanation and example explain Strunk & White's Chapter V (Rule #11).

Writers should not clutter their work with adverbs and explanatory notes because readers do not need excessive explanation. One common mistake is using an adverb after the word *said*. Most times that adverb is not needed and the wording turns into an unnecessary annoyance.

> Incorrect: Hector said begrudgingly to Reginald that he hoped it rained during the picnic.
>
> Correct: Hector said to Reginald that he hoped it rained during the picnic.

Avoid awkward adverbs

Adverbs are created by adding *ly* to the end of words. For example, *over* is changed to *overly* and *just* is changed to *justly*. Writing, however, is more effective when adverbs are not used. In general, a word that is not used verbally should not be used in writing.

Incorrect: Yolanda is overly sensitive.

Correct: Yolanda is over sensitive.

Incorrect: Martha looked sickly.

Correct: Martha looked sick.

This explanation and example explain Strunk & White's Chapter V (Rule #12).

Clearly identify the person speaking

Readers should always know who is speaking. If they are confused about who is speaking, then they are forced to reread what is written and might eventually stop making the effort to do so.

Incorrect: The massacre started in the morning, Jack said to Jill, and ended at noon.

Correct: Jack said to Jill that the massacre started in the morning and ended at noon.

This explanation and example explain Strunk & White's Chapter V (Rule #13).

Also, a sentence should not be awkwardly interrupted. The break should be the same as in a verbal conversation.

Incorrect: "Furthermore, a person," he said, "should not go to London without an umbrella."

Correct: "Furthermore," he said, "a person should not go to London without an umbrella."

Do not use fancy words

Writers should not use a complex word when a simple word works just as well because the simple word is more

This
explanation
and
example
explain
Strunk &
White's
Chapter V
(Rule #14).

easily understood. There is often a fine line between complex words and simple words, so an effort might be required to make the correct choice. Factors affecting this choice include the education, age, social status, and career of the readers.

Incorrect: Team number one consisted of ten employees with heterogeneous work experience, while team number two consisted of eight employees with homogenous work experience.

Correct: Team number one consisted of ten employees with different work experience, while team number two consisted of eight employees with similar work experience.

This
explanation
and
example
explain
Strunk &
White's
Chapter V
(Rule #15).

Avoid dialect

Dialect in writing refers to spelling, grammar, and pronunciation of words that have specific meanings to certain groups of readers. It should be used sparingly in writing because it confuses readers who do not understand the meaning.

Incorrect: Jolene said hello to Jim in the morning, hi to Roger in the afternoon, and howdy to Regina in the evening.

Correct: Jolene said hello to Jim in the morning, hello to Roger in the afternoon, and hello to Regina in the evening.

If a writer does use dialect, then it should be consistent throughout the work.

If a food is initially referred to as a *crayfish*, then do not call it a *crawdad* or *shrimp* later in the writing.

Clarity is critical

Writing must be clear to express the writer's intent. Without clarity, communication is lost, confusion results, and readers lose interest. Sometimes this can be done by breaking one long sentence into two short sentences.

> Incorrect: He walked into the bar, gave the bartender a fifty dollar bill, and asked for three bottles of beer and two glasses of wine and, after he consumed all five drinks, was unable to drive home.
>
> Correct: He walked into the bar, gave the bartender a fifty dollar bill, and asked for three bottles of beer and two glasses of wine. After he consumed all five drinks, he was unable to drive home.

This explanation and example explain Strunk & White's Chapter V (Rule #16).

Avoid injecting opinions

Everyone has an opinion, but those opinions differ based on perceptions and situations. People should not inject their opinions into their writing in order to avoid appearing biased or egotistical. Additionally, readers feel disrespected or offended when they read something that differs from their own viewpoints.

> Incorrect: She was obviously a democrat based on her overwhelming concern for poor people.
>
> Correct: She might have been a democrat based on her concern for poor people.

This explanation and example explain Strunk & White's Chapter V (Rule #17).

Avoid using figures of speech

Figures of speech are words or phrases used in a non-literal sense for a vivid effect, and they should not be used in formal writing. For example, someone might say, "She is slower than molasses in January." This means she is slow when she works on tasks, but it does not mean she moves slower than molasses flows in cold weather.

> Incorrect: Charles can't walk and chew gum at the same time.
>
> Correct: Charles lacks the ability to multi-task.

This explanation and example explain Strunk & White's Chapter V (Rule #18).

Avoid shortcuts at the expense of clarity

This explanation and example explain Strunk & White's Chapter V (Rule #19).

Writing shortcuts should not be taken if clarity is jeopardized. Do not use initials or acronyms for names of companies, job classifications, programs, or organizations because readers might not understand.

Incorrect: Candice is an IO psychologist who works at GM studying OB.

Correct: Candice is an industrial/organizational psychologist who works at General Motors studying organizational behavior.

Avoid foreign languages

This explanation and example explain Strunk & White's Chapter V (Rule #20).

Foreign languages should not be used in writing because most people do not understand the words. This lack of comprehension results in a loss of communication, and readers do not gain anything other than frustration. People are confused when something is written in a language that they do not understand, so stick to a language that is germane to readers.

Incorrect: Timothy said *Danke* after Peggy gave him Michele's address.

Correct: Timothy said thank you after Peggy gave him Michele's address.

Avoid offbeat wording

This explanation and example explain Strunk & White's Chapter V (Rule #21).

Standard words and phrases should be used in writing because offbeat words and phrases go out of style, are forgotten, or lose meaning. When any of these happen, readers do not understand the intent of the message or they find the writing archaic. Examples include "gnarly" and "cool cat."

Incorrect: Rick and Shaun had a groovy time at the concert.

Correct: Rick and Shaun had a good time at the concert.

Part VI:
Rules for Writing Essays

This chapter includes examples of a variety of Strunk & White's Chapter I and Chapter II rules used when writing essays.

Essay #1

People in the United States are choosing not to smoke. This is not surprising based on the wealth of information available on the negative effects of smoking. The Center for Disease Control (2008) found that less than 20 percent of the population smokes, which is the lowest percentage since the 1960s. More encouraging is the fact that there is no indication that this downward trend is going to change.

Research clearly indicates people associate lung cancer with smoking (Martin, 2005). Aside from medical study findings, the obvious correlation comes from the inhalation of smoke directly into the lungs. The resulting closed capsule environment is perfect for carcinogens to destroy human health. Watching a loved one suffer or die from lung cancer leaves a lasting impression on many people, and smoking is often a big part of that picture.

Lung cancer is not the only cancer that results from smoking. The Surgeon General's report (2004) found harmful linkages with the stomach, cervix, pancreas, and kidney. These diseases are treatable in some instances, but in other cases they are fatal. This deadly concern caused the government to invest considerable time and effort into publicly attacking smoking, and people decided to listen.

The government and other public interest groups have gradually changed the American perception of smoking (Sauls, 2011). It has been

Ownership of a noun not ending in s.

Whenever a sentence contains a series of items, place a comma after each element.

A comma should be used when a conjunction introduces an independent clause.

many years since the Marlboro man made his last television appearance, and <u>movie actors and actresses appear out of place with a cigarette dangling from their mouths.</u> Thankfully, tobacco is taboo in many people's minds; and the end result is a reduction in the smoking population.

Fewer and fewer Americans are smoking. Medical studies have <u>convinced them that tobacco products result in adverse health issues,</u> and cancer is the main culprit. Public campaigns mounted against smoking have been effective, causing people to refrain from lighting up during their drive to work, after dinner, or during a good conversation. This is great because decreased smoking equates to a national decline in disease and death. Quite simply, people are getting it... before it gets them!

> Two independent clauses cannot be connected with a comma alone. There must be a comma and a coordinating conjunction or a semicolon. This example demonstrates the use of a comma and coordinating conjunction (and).

> The word "thankfully" creates a positive tone for the sentence.

> An example of active voice writing where the subject shows the action of the verb.

Essay #2

Farm animals in the United States are dying at an early age. Chickens are not living long enough to lay eggs, and hogs and cattle are perishing before they are old enough to breed and reproduce.

Subject and verbs must agree in number and person.

Early death rates in farm animals are the result of several different factors. Air pollution from cities is finding its way into rural communities. Factories in urban areas are churning out smoke that is damaging to the environment for miles around. Animals need clean air for healthy living, and it is not always available.

Contaminated river water is also an issue. Tainted water from industrial areas flows into rural communities where it is used by farmers for their livestock. Despite environmental rules and regulations, some companies still use rivers for discharge of waste.

Lastly, there is overcrowding of animals being raised on farms. Gone are the days when animals roamed freely on open ranges. Tough economic times have forced farmers to make more money using less space, and this acts as a catalyst for spreading disease.

Nonrestrictive elements are not needed in order to understand the context of the sentence, so they are set off with commas.

American farmers are losing their livestock at a young age due to the industrial waste, land shortages, and the economy. The United States government, normally slow to react, needs to create stricter laws for pollution to curb this devastation. The government also needs to provide financial aid to the farmers to prevent them from going out of business. The time for action is now, or farming might just become another industry that is outsourced to foreign countries.

Essay #3

Paying college athletes has recently become a hot topic of discussion. Some people believe college sports should remain an amateur competition where sportsmanship is at the forefront and players are not monetarily compensated. Others argue that it is time to pay players because the college sports world is vastly different since the rules were established many years ago. I believe the times have changed, and so should athlete compensation.

First and foremost, college athletes bring in huge revenue for their schools as noted by ESPN. Millions of dollars are made from advertisers, fans, students, and alumni. The schools profit while the players do 100 percent of the work. This is simply not fair.

Another unfair aspect is the fact that most college athletes will not play professionally. This might be the only opportunity they have to get paid for their skills. The current financial situation is a win-lose. The universities win, and the athletes lose.

If college athletes did get paid, the only people who would lose are the ones who should. Payments from dishonest boosters, recruiters, and agents would be eliminated. Right now, these individuals have a great opportunity to illegally funnel money to players in exchange for wins or future favors. If the athletes were paid by the schools, then they might stop accepting money from unscrupulous people.

Some sports fans argue that college sports should promote amateur competition only, and the athletes should not be compensated. While this viewpoint

A topic sentence is placed at the beginning of a paragraph, and it states the main idea of the paragraph.

Emphatic and definite words are generally placed at the end of a sentence.

Example of a parallel sentence where words are placed using a consistent style/structure.

has some validity, it is not fair. The players bring in huge revenue for their schools and might never have the opportunity to make money professionally. Unscrupulous individuals also profit illegally when the players do not get paid. It is hard to determine exactly how much money athletes should make, but there needs to be some type of financial reward system in place. Maybe a payment cap is the answer.

Part VII:
Bonus Section

To further expand on Strunk and White's book, we have added a bonus section that includes detailed instructions on how to set up a document using Microsoft Word. While many academic institutions and employers require different formats, we've selected *The American Psychological Association* (APA) for a paper example. This format is very commonly used throughout many academic disciplines and employment industries.

The following are specific instructions on how to set up a document for APA writing format using the various versions of Microsoft Word.

*Note: The first set of instructions applies to using Microsoft Word *prior* to the Word 2007 version. The second set of instructions applies to using versions of Microsoft Word from 2007 to the current version.

Utilizing Microsoft Word *(Versions prior to 2007)*

The following are specific instructions on how to set up a document for APA format using Microsoft Word.

Margins

All margins (top, bottom, and sides) should be set at a minimum of one inch. Microsoft Word allows the user to set the margin at a default of one inch. To do so, follow the guidelines below:

1. Under FILE, select PAGE SETUP.

2. Select MARGINS tab and type 1" at TOP, BOTTOM, LEFT, and RIGHT boxes. Click OK.

Alignment/Line Spacing

All documents following APA guidelines are required to be aligned left and double-spaced throughout the entire document. Be sure not to include additional spacing between paragraphs, headings, *etc.* To set the default, follow these guidelines:

1. Place the cursor at the start of the document, select FORMAT.

2. Under FORMAT, select PARAGRAPH.

3. Under PARAGRAPH, set ALIGNMENT to LEFT.

4. Under PARAGRAPH, set LINE SPACING to DOUBLE. Click OK.

Font Type and Size

The preferred font type is Times New Roman. Additionally, APA requires the font size to be 12 point.

This is an example of 12-point Times New Roman.

To set both the font size and style using Word, do the following:

1. Under FORMAT, select FONT.

2. Under FONT, select Times New Roman.

3. Under SIZE, select 12.

Paragraph Indentation

All papers typed in APA format require paragraphs to be indented one-half inch. This can easily be accomplished by striking TAB on the keyboard.

To set tab to the one-half inch default, do the following:

1. Under FORMAT, select PARAGRAPH.

2. Under PARAGRAPH, select TABS.

3. Under TABS, set DEFAULT TAB STOPS at .5".

Hanging Indents

To set the hanging indent feature, do the following:

1. Under FORMAT, select PARAGRAPH.

2. Under SPECIAL, choose HANGING. Click OK.

Johnson, L. R. (2005). *People who live in glass houses should not throw stones.* Chicago, IL: Alleman and Anderson Books.

Page Header

Beginning on the very first page (title page) and running continually throughout the APA document, a page header is utilized. The page header should appear one-half inch down from the top margin. It includes the running head flush left and the page number flush right. On the title page, the page header consists of the words *Running head* (the *R* in *Running* is capitalized) followed by a colon and the title of the paper in all capital letters. Subsequent pages should *not* use the words *Running head.* There is a maximum of 50 characters (including spaces) after the colon. If the title encompasses more than 50 characters, then only major words should be used. This can be accomplished using the HEADER AND FOOTER function.

1. Under VIEW, select HEADER AND FOOTER. The cursor will appear flush left in the header box.

2. Type Running head: TITLE OF YOUR PAPER.

Note: The *R* is uppercase; the *h* is lowercase. Also, the actual title of the paper should be in all uppercase letters.

3. Tab twice to move to the right aligned position.

4. Select the # icon in HEADER AND FOOTER box.

5. Select CLOSE.

6. Move the cursor to the end of the title page.

7. Click INSERT then BREAK.

8. Under SECTION, choose NEXT PAGE.

Note: At this point, a second page containing the same page header as the first page will appear (except the page number will be 2 instead of 1).

9. Under VIEW, select HEADER AND FOOTER. The cursor will appear flush left in the header box.

10. On the HEADER/FOOTER toolbar, click SAME AS PREVIOUS to break the connection with the previous header.

11. Delete the words *Running head:* and introductory space(s). Click CLOSE.

Utilizing Microsoft Word (Versions 2007-Present)

The following are specific instructions for setting up an APA document using Microsoft Word 2007 to present.

Margins

All margins (top, bottom, and sides) should be set at a minimum of one inch. Microsoft Word allows the user to set the margin at a default of one inch. To do so, follow the guidelines below:

1. Select PAGE LAYOUT from the ribbon tabs.

2. Select the MARGINS icon.

3. Click on NORMAL.

Alignment/Line Spacing

All documents following APA guidelines are required to be aligned left and double-spaced throughout the entire document. Be sure not to include additional spacing between paragraphs, headings, *etc.* To set the default, follow these guidelines:

1. Select HOME from the ribbon tabs.
2. Select the PARAGRAPH window (by clicking the icon to the right of the word *paragraph*).
3. Under ALIGNMENT, select LEFT.
4. Under LINE SPACING, select DOUBLE.
5. Under SPACING set both BEFORE and AFTER to 0 pt. or simply click *Don't add space between paragraphs of the same style.*
6. Click OK.

Font Type and Size

The preferred font type is Times New Roman. Additionally, APA requires the font size to be 12 point.

This is an example of 12-point Times New Roman.

1. Select HOME from the ribbon tabs.
2. Select the FONT window (by clicking the icon to the right of the word *font*).
3. Select Times New Roman.
4. Select SIZE of 12. Click OK.

Paragraph Indentation

All papers typed in APA format require paragraphs to be indented one-half inch. This can easily be accomplished by striking TAB on the keyboard.

Hanging Indents

To set the hanging indent feature, do the following:

1. Select HOME from the ribbon tabs.

2. Select the PARAGRAPH window (by clicking the icon to the right of the word *paragraph*), and select the INDENTS AND SPACING tab.

3. Under SPECIAL, choose HANGING. Under BY, select .5". Click OK.

Page Header

Beginning on the very first page (title page) and running continually throughout the APA document, a page header is utilized. The page header should appear one-half inch down from the top margin. It includes the running head flush left and the page number flush right. On the title page, the page header consists of the words *Running head* (the *R* in *Running* is capitalized) followed by a colon and the title of the paper in all capital letters. Subsequent pages should *not* use the words *Running head.* There is a maximum of 50 characters (including spaces) after the colon. If the title encompasses more than 50 characters, then only major words should be used. This can be accomplished using the HEADER AND FOOTER function.

1. Select INSERT from the ribbon tabs.

2. Select HEADER.

3. Select EDIT HEADER.

4. Type Running head: TITLE OF YOUR PAPER.

Note: The *R* is uppercase; the *h* is lowercase. Also, the actual title of the paper should be in all uppercase letters.

5. Tab twice to move to the right aligned position.

6. Select PAGE NUMBER option.

7. Select CURRENT POSITION.

8. Select PLAIN NUMBER. This will right-align the page number.

9. Select CLOSE HEADER AND FOOTER (located in the upper right-hand corner).

Note: Steps 10 through 15 show how to create a section break between the title page and second page in order to change the page header. Step 16 shows how to alter the page header on page two and subsequent pages.

10. Place your cursor at the end of the text on the title page.

11. Select PAGE LAYOUT from the ribbon tabs.

12. On the PAGE SETUP menu, click on BREAKS.

13. Under SECTION BREAKS, select NEXT PAGE.

14. Click on the page header on page 2.

15. Click on LINK TO PREVIOUS to de-select it.

16. Delete the words *Running head:* and introductory space(s) and click CLOSE HEADER AND FOOTER.

Title Page

The title page of the document should include the following:

- Page header: Running head is flush left; page number is flush right.

- Title of the paper, student's name, and name of college or university (centered on the page).

The Running head will appear .5" from the top of the page. The *R* is uppercase, while the *h* is lowercase. After the words *Running head*, there is a colon, one space, and the title of the paper typed in all uppercase letters. Note that this is the only part of the APA document that will appear in all uppercase lettering. Also, there is a limit of 50 maximum total characters starting after the colon…counting spaces. It may be necessary to use only main words of the title.

Running head: MOTIVATING EMPLOYEES

The page header will appear one-half inch from the top margin on each page. At the left margin, the words *Running head* should appear, followed by a colon and the title of the paper (typed in all uppercase lettering). This title should be 50 characters maximum, including spaces. The page number should appear in the page header flush right. The *header* feature in Word should be utilized when establishing the page header.

The title of the paper, student's name, and name of college or university should be typed in that order and be centered on the title page.

Levels of Headings

When a document requires the use of headings, the following five levels should be utilized (*Publication Manual of the American Psychological Association* (6th edition), 2010, pp. 62-63):

Centered, Boldface, Uppercase and Lowercase Heading
(Level One)

Flush Left, Boldface, Uppercase and Lowercase Heading
(Level Two)

>**Indented, boldface, lowercase paragraph heading ending with a period.**
(Level Three)

>*__Indented, boldface, italicized, lowercase paragraph heading ending with a period.__*
(Level Four)

>*Indented, italicized, lowercase paragraph heading ending with a period.*
(Level Five)

Note: In levels three, four, and five, capitalize only the first letter of the first word.

Note: In levels three, four, and five, the paragraph begins on the same line as the heading.

Index

T

U

W

www.ingramcontent.com/pod-product-compliance
Lightning Source LLC
Chambersburg PA
CBHW022121280326

41933CB00007B/487